Cape Cod
Shipwrecks

"Graveyard of the Atlantic"

Theodore Parker Burbank

Shipwrecks on

Cape Cod

"Graveyard of the Atlantic"

Theodore Parker Burbank

Salty Pilgrim Press
www.SaltyPilgim.com

ISBN 978-1-935616-07-8

Cover design:

G. Scott B.
Sunshine Joy
Pawtucket, R.I.

Cover Artwork: 1854 Painting by Ivan Aivazovsky

For additional copies or more information, please contact:

Salty Pilgrim Press
17 Causeway Street
Millis, MA 02054 USA
1 508 794-1200
captain@saltypilgrim.com

Second Edition

Printed in the USA

Forward

Cape Cod is the bared and bended arm of Massachusetts; the shoulder is at Buzzard's Bay; the elbow or crazy bone is at Cape Mallebarre (Chatham); the wrist at Truro; and the sandy fist at Provincetown. . . boxing with the northeast storms, and, ever and anon, heaving her Atlantic adversary from the lap of the earth.

HENRY DAVID THOREAU

Danger

The Shoals are so numerous about this locality that descriptions would be useless and their enumeration would only tend to confuse.

No stranger should attempt their navigation, except by Main Ship Channel, without a pilot.

Even with the most perfect chart it is extremely hazardous.

(Note from Cape Cod sailing chart 1859)

Table of Contents

Watery Grave to Thousands

Thousands of Shipwrecks off Cape Cod

So many ships have piled up on the hidden sand bars off the coast between Chatham and Provincetown that those fifty miles of sea have been called an "ocean graveyard" containing an estimated 3,500 shipwrecks including that of the *Whydah Gally*, the famed pirate ship of Black Sam Bellamy that went down with over 4.5 tons of gold, silver, jewels and other treasures off Marconi Beach.

In fact, between Truro and Wellfleet alone, according to the U.S. Lifesaving Service, there had been more than 1,000 wrecks from 1850 until the Cape Cod Canal was opened in 1918.

Ship Ashore!

When a storm struck the Cape in the early days, no one was surprised to hear the alarm: "Ship ashore! All hands perishing!" The townspeople would turn out on the beach, but usually the surf was too high for them to attempt a rescue; and by the time the storm was over, there was usually no one alive to rescue.

The First Recorded Wreck

The first recorded wreck was the *Sparrow-Hawk* which ran aground at Orleans in 1626 after successfully the sailing more than 3,000 miles from England to Cape Cod. The 25 people aboard the tiny 29 ft craft were able to get ashore safely, and the ship was repaired. But, before it could set sail, the ship was sunk by another storm, buried in the sand, and wasn't seen for over two hundred years. In 1863, after storms had shifted the sands again, the skeleton of the *Sparrow-Hawk* reappeared briefly. So the ocean takes and gives back and takes again. (The ribs of the ship are now on display at the Cape Cod Maritime Museum).

Sparrow-Hawk ribs 1863

An Ocean Graveyard

"Most Treacherous Coast in the World"

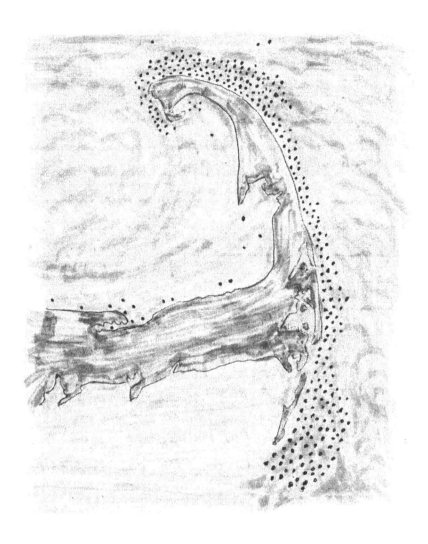

*The Dots, Indicating Locations of Some of the
Major Shipwrecks along Cape Cod Shores,
Illustrate why the Cape earned the Reputation as
the "Graveyard of the Atlantic"*

Graveyard of the Atlantic – Why?

Why is this Beautiful Coast so Deadly?

The stretch of the Cape Cod coast from Provincetown to Monomoy Island was infamously known as the *Graveyard of the Atlantic* for centuries and for two major reasons.

Reason #1 – <u>Peaked Hill Bar</u>

The chart shows the shallow water extending far out into the Atlantic with a trough of deep water and then the shallows of Peaked Hill Bar.

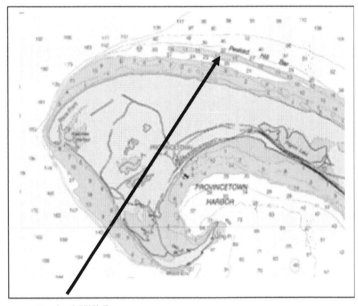

Peaked Hill Bar

In a north east blow, ships would enter the trough with the wind behind them and not be able to tack or navigate out of the deadly triangle. Others, being a mile or more at sea, were surprised to find themselves in a beach like surf and then, aground on the shifting sand of Peaked Hill Bar.

Reason #2 – __Monomoy Shoals__

Named Cape Malabar (Cape of Evil Bars) by the French in the early 1600s

One of the most dangerous choke points in a trip along the New England coast are the turns you have to make to avoid Pollack Bar and the shoals off Monomy and Chatham. The narrow channel between shoals has been called a gauntlet with ships guided at night by following the lights of floating lighthouses or lightships.

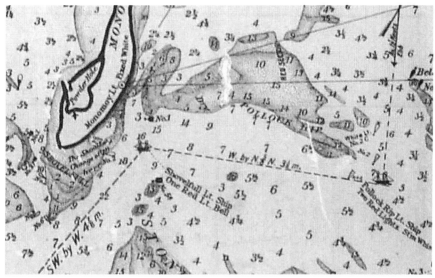

The gauntlet around Monomoy's shoals

Monomoy, once a peninsula about eight miles long reaching southward from Chatham at the elbow of Cape Cod, has been split by erosion and storms into two islands known as North and South Monomoy. The constantly shifting sands of South Monomoy have placed about a mile between Monomoy lighthouse and the shore.

With Nantucket Sound to the west, and the frigid Atlantic Ocean to the east, dangerous "rips" where the two come together over shallow shoals and bars have led to hundreds of shipwrecks, and the early French sailors name of Cape Malabar—the "Cape of Evil Bars."

Add other Factors

Shifting Shoals, Strong Currents and Treacherous Weather

"There is no other part of the world, perhaps," wrote, the director of the United States Coast and Geodetic Survey in 1869, "where tides of such very small rise and fall are accompanied by such strong currents running far out to sea."

A vessel can be a mile or more off shore and run aground on a sandbar that had not been there when the GPS course was set sometime earlier. Imagine if you can, navigating without modern day electronics, depth finders, radar, radio and the like and imagine your only source of power is unpredictable and uncontrollable wind in your sails.

Now – place yourself inside a dense fog sailing in a small circle of visibility with only a compass to guide you and knowing all to well that treacherous shifting sands are waiting to grasp your ship and perhaps, send you and your crew to an early and watery grave.

Even worse – put yourself aboard a sailing vessel in mid-winter during a blinding blizzard with hurricane force winds churning up mountainous seas that crash across your decks. The temperatures are below zero and the snow heavy and wet.

The freezing snow clings and builds up on every mast, spa, rope, cable and sail making the vessel top heavy and difficult to handle. Walking on the decks is next to impossible. You and your crew tie lifelines around your waist or climb into the rigging where you tie yourself to the mast or a spar.

Under such conditions masts will break, canvass sails can tear asunder, steering can become impossible and your vessel can readily broach (come sideways to the seas) and be capsized by a mountainous wave.

Combine all of these factors and it is small wonder that Cape Cod earned the title of "Graveyard of the Atlantic."

Peaked Hills Bar Historic District

Watery Grave of a Countless Number of Sailors

The waters and beaches of the 1,500-acre Peaked Hill Bars

The beach at Peaked Hills Bars Historic District

Historic District in the Seashore in Provincetown and Truro are where thousands of sailors and countless ships met their demise.

One of the 19 Dune Shacks in Peaked Hills Bars Historic District

Today there are only 19 Dune Shacks in the entire park. The shacks are leased back to the Seashore, and lessees pay a modest fee annually with a promise they will maintain these rustic structures.

6

Cape Cod Lighthouses

Aids to Navigation Save Lives

Beginning in 1857, lighthouses were erected to serve as beacons and to aid ships in avoiding danger. Highland Light (or Cape Cod Light) is the oldest and tallest on the Cape, and remains as one of a number of working lighthouses on Cape Cod and the Islands.

Most of Cape Cod's lighthouses are operated by the U.S. Coast Guard with some exceptions such as the Nauset Light, which was decommissioned in 1996 and is now maintained by the Nauset Light Preservation Society under the auspices of Cape Cod National Seashore. These lighthouses are frequently photographed symbols of Cape Cod.

Highland Light circa 1950

In 1996, both the Highland Light and Nauset Light were moved, because they were each at risk of being lost to the encroaching seas. The Highland Light, then 110 ft from the ocean, was moved 450 ft to the west, and the Nauset Light, a mere 37 ft from the ocean, was moved 300 ft west.

The 18 lighthouses of Cape Cod include:
> **Lower Cape:** Long Point Light, Wood End Light, Race Point Light, Highland Light, Nauset Light, Three Sisters of Nauset, Mayo Beach Light, Billingsgate Island Light, Chatham Light, Monomoy Point Light, Stage Harbor Light
> **Mid Cape:** Sandy Neck Light, Hyannis Harbor Light, Lewis Bay Light (or Hyannis Inner Harbor Light, also private), Bishop and Clerks Light, West Dennis Light (formerly the Bass River Light)
> **Upper Cape**: Nobska Light, Wing's Neck Light (privately owned)

Cape Cod Lightships

Floating Lighthouses

Cape Cod waters have more than an average share of lightships and the chart below showing the Cape's many sand bars vividly illustrates why.

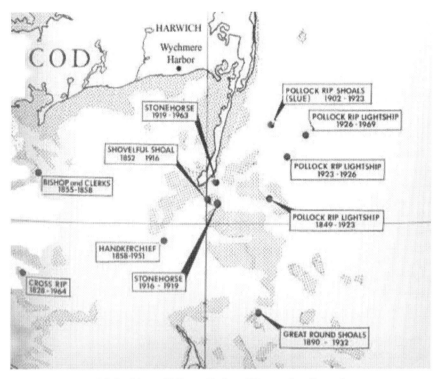

Lightships off Cape Cod and Nantucket Sound

Lightship Falls Prey to Ice Pack

Feb. 1, 1918 – LV-6 Floats Away with Ice Pack

During a mid winter thaw on February 1st, 1918 the ice sheet began to move and the forces of ice and tide against the 63 year old Lightship parted its riding gear. The powerless vessel was spotted on February 5th by the Great Point Light keeper east of the Great Round Shoal lightship station heading eastward, a captive in the moving ice.

LV-6 Lost with all hands

Later, an all out search for the drifting ship produced no sign of the vessel and was presumed sunk with all hands. They were all residents of the Cape. In 1987, a lightship bell presumed from LV-6 was recovered off Nauset Beach.

Lightship LV-73 Sank During Hurricane - 1944

The Vineyard Sound Light vessel became an unintended tragedy in 1944, unrelated to war, the LV-73 which had once served duty at this station for 20 years sank in the September 14th Hurricane. 19 years later, it was discovered by divers that hull plating where the storm anchor had hung at the bow, were stove in. Normally the 3 to 5 ton mushroom anchor is let go in intense weather. The crew unable to accomplish this, led to high seas slamming the anchor through the hull and sinking the ship.

Let the Bell Toll

An earlier lightship, one of four that served at the Handkerchief Shoals, Lightship LV-4 stood duty off Harwich Port a record 58 years (1858 - 1916) and used a 958 lbs hand operated bell as a fog signal. One can only imagine the endless monotony of each crew member on his four-hour anchor watch striking the ships bell for five seconds every minute in thick weather (considered rain, fog, snow, sleet).

Salvaging the Wrecks

Waste not, Want not – It was a Business

After a wreck, townspeople would come out with their horses and carts and haul away whatever the ship had been carrying. Then they would dismantle the ship piece by piece and cart away the valuable lumber. Many of the old Cape Cod houses, churches and Inns contain lumber salvaged from these wrecks.

Salvagers assemble on the beach

Shipwrecks were so common on the Cape that the profession of "Wrecker" was established. They were the recyclers of their day.

Wreckers stripping the ship

Owners of the wreck paid the local people to salvage their cargo and the wreckers to salvage the ship. Often the local people simply went on the theory that finders were keepers.

"Beachcombers" was another term used to describe more casual salvagers of wrecks along Cape beaches.

After the Wreckers have completed their work

Mooncussers

Lured Ships onto the Beach

Mooncussers, or mooners for short, were a nefarious version of wreckers or beachcombers. Wreckers would contract their services with the owners of the wrecked ship and salvage all that was possible before the next high surf claimed the ship. Mooners didn't want to wait for a storm to produce a wreck so they would try to cause a wreck to happen.

Mooncussers were so called for they required a dark moonless night in order to successfully lure a passing ship onto the beach. They would stand on the shore swinging a lantern to simulate a ship's stern light.

Mooncussers attempting to lure a ship ashore

Ships at sea seeking a safe passage through the treacherous waters off the tip of the Cape would change course, assuming their navigation was off and follow what they believed to be a ship familiar with the local waters. Instead of safe passage they would run aground and the ship plundered by the Mooncussers.

The Mooncusser's activity was so prevalent and well known that in Rudyard Kipling's book "Captains Courageous", there is a passage. . . *"Ye scrabbletowners, Ye Chatham wreckers! Git oout with your brick in your stocking!"*

Rescuing Sailors

You Have to Go Out but You Don't Have to Return

In the early 1800s, there was an average of two wrecks every month during the winter. The loss of life seemed especially sad when a sailor managed to get ashore on a winter night only to freeze to death after he got there.

In 1797, the Massachusetts Humane Society started putting up huts along the most dangerous and isolated sections of the Massachusetts coast in the hope that stranded sailors would find them and take shelter. It was not, however, until 1872, that a really efficient lifesaving service was put into operation by the United States government. Stations were erected every five miles on the beach with a "halfway house" in between.

Surfmen would walk 2 1/2 miles to the halfway house, exchange tickets (proof they had made the trip) and return to their respective stations regardless of the weather. In fact, it was most important that they were out in the very worst weather for it was then that vessels would be most likely be in trouble and in need of their services.

Halfway house on the beach north of Chatham Light - Circa 1900

Six or seven surfmen and a keeper lived in each station and kept a continuous lookout. At night, two men from each station walked the beach on patrol.

When a ship in distress was sighted, a red signal was fired to let the crew at sea know they'd been seen. If the sea permitted, the surfmen launched their special surfboats - some equipped with air chambers (to help keep them afloat), cork fenders (to keep them from being smashed against the sinking ship), and righting lines (to use in case they capsized).

If they could not get out by boat and if the shipwreck was near enough to shore, the lifesaving team would attempt a rescue from the beach using a breeches bouy to pull the sinking crew ashore, one by one.

A "Breeches Bouy" was a basket like rig, attached to a rope that was suspended on a pulley and rope strung high over the water. The lifesavers used a Lyle gun (small cannon) to fire a line to the floundering ship. The double line with pulley was then secured to the mast of the ship and the other end to a structure anchored in the sand on the beach.

Then the breeches buoy was sent over the ropes to the ship. One sailor from the sinking ship at a time would climb into the breeches buoy and be pulled to shore. The breeches-buoy would then go back for the next rescue as so it would go until the last sailor had been rescued.

A Winslow Homer painting depicting a Breeches Bouy rescue

There were 12 Lifesaving Stations from Provincetown to Monomoy Point:

Woods End,	Peaked Hill Bars	High Head	Highlands
Pamet River	Cahoon Hollow	Nauset	Orleans
Old Harbor	Chatham	Monomoy	Monomoy Point

Lifesaving Station Locations

Station and major shipwreck locations

The Lifesavers

Selfless Heroes

The surfmen who manned the lifesaving stations along the most dangerous winter coast in the world were known and respected for their gallant deeds, enduring bravery and their successes in saving lives, all over the world.

From Wood End at Provincetown to Monomoy at Chatham every night, regardless of the weather, they would walk the exposed beaches on the lookout for endangered ships.

The crew of the Highland Lifesaving Station

The surfmen were paid $65 a month (early 1900). The harsh conditions took a heavy toll on the men's health causing many to have to retire early.

Some of the Wrecks off Highland Lifesaving Station

Twenty three of the hundreds of ships lost here

Isaac Small, who was stationed at Highland Light in 1861, wrote "the whitened bones of hundreds of dead sailors lie buried in the drifting sands of this storm beaten coast." Of 3,000 Cape wrecks, these are a few lost off Wellfleet:

Whydah, 1717	*Cactus*, 1847	*Cambria*, 1849
Franklin, 1849	*St Cloud*, 1863	*White Squall*, 1868*
Kilhorn, 1874	*Florida*, 1890	*Gray Eagle*, 1890
Jason, 1893	*Messenger*, 1894	*Fearing*, 1896
Welcome, 1896	*Heisler*, 1897	*Empire State*, 1899
Holden, 1899	*Smuggler*, 1899	*Black Bird*, 1900
Campbell, 1912	*Mead*, 1913	*Castagna*, 1914
Hickey, 1927	*Paulmino*, 1959	

- The White Squall was returning from China when she ran aground

The Messenger 1894

Charles A Campbell 1912

The Cape Cod Canal

The Widest Sea Level Canal in the World

Background

In 1623 Myles Standish of the Plymouth Colony was the first to propose the construction of a Canal across the isthmus. The two rivers the Manamet River and the Scusset River were separated by a short stretch suggesting the construction of a canal was a possibility. Nearly three hundred years later, after many proposals and surveys, it would become a reality.

The Indians had been using this Inland Passage for centuries. They would paddle their canoes back and forth from Cape Cod Bay to Buzzard's Bay using the Manamet Portage between the Scusset River and Manamet River. The Indian name "Manamet" translates to "Trail of the burden carriers" or

Proposed canal route of 1825

portage.

The Indians ability to trade with other tribes was greatly facilitated by this passage. The tradition of Native American trading in this area was to be continued by the Pilgrims when the Plymouth Colony established the Aptucxet Trading Post on the banks of the Manamet River, now the Cape Cod Canal, in 1627.

The General Court of Massachusetts considered the first formal proposal to build the canal in 1697 but took no action. In 1776 George Washington ordered the Continental Army to conduct an intensive feasibility survey. More studies would follow, 1791, 1803, 1818, 1824–1830, and 1860 and finally construction of the canal began on June 22, 1909. The Canal was officially opened, with great fanfare, seventeen days before the opening of the Panama Canal.

Graveyard of the Atlantic No More

At the end of the 1800s the Corp of Engineers estimates shipwrecks, on the outer Cape, were occurring at the alarming rate of one major wreck every two weeks! The loss of life and treasure was catastrophic thereby rightfully

A typical sight prior to the Canal's construction

earning the waters off the Cape the name - *Graveyard of the Atlantic*. A reputation well deserved.

The hundreds, if not thousands, of lives saved by the safer sailing route offered by the Canal must be considered the most valuable contribution made by the Canal. The Canal route does save 125 miles, much time and considerable fuel making trade with New York and the ports to the south more profitable and secure. Over 20,000 vessels of all types use the Canal annually.

Strategic Element of America's National Security System

In 1918, a German submarine attacked American shipping off Nauset Beach sinking four barges and damaging the tug *Perth Ambo* setting her afire. President Woodrow Wilson reacted by ordering the takeover, operation and eventually widening and deepening of the Canal to assure the safety of coastwise shipping.

The Canal became the *"Gateway to America's Intracoastal Waterway."* A Navy Department spokesman said "The Cape

Safe passage through the Canal

Cod Canal, which permits shipping of all kinds to freely pass between the waters of Cape Cod Bay and Long Island Sound, becomes a strategic feature that cannot be overestimated.

Shipping of all kinds can freely use it without exposure in time of war to attack by enemy forces. In peace time it affords a comfortable and convenient passage during weather that often renders passage by the outside route hazardous."

During World War II, in 1939, British ships in camouflage used the Canal to avoid German submarines. With the threat of German U-boats, the Canal was on high alert. Although

The United States did not participate in World War II for two more years, the war came early to Cape Cod.

In 1942, the Canal's operation was placed in the hands of the United States Coast Guard. The army manned the coast while the Navy maintained offshore patrols.

Within the first six months of war (January to July), five United Nations vessels fell prey to German submarines in the Cape Cod area. Later on in the war, the Germans successfully added three more to their list. In contrast, one hundred ships were sunk in the Eastern Sea Frontier. If it were not for the protection of the Cape Cod Canal the number of ships lost would have been much higher.

Canal side memorial to all US Submariners
that are "Still on Patrol"

Castagna - 1914

One of the last shipwrecks before the Canal opened later that year

Captain and Three Sailors in Rigging Frozen

Lifesavers, as Storm Moderates, Get Out to the Italian Bark Wrecked on Cape Cod and Learn Why Lines Shot Across Her Deck Were Not Pulled In

MEN TOO BENUMBED TO AID SELVES

Wellfleet, Mass. Feb. 17 – Five men perished when the Italian bark *Castagna* struck on the outer bar a mile a half south of the Cahoon's Hollow life saving station today.

The mate and seven seamen, all badly frostbitten and nearly unconscious from exposure, were brought ashore by lifeboats. The frozen corpses of captain Garva and three sailors were left in the rigging where the men had lashed themselves during the hours of darkness to avoid being carried overboard by the seas that swept the deck. The fifth victim died in the surf boat

The Castagna the day following the storm

on way to land.

The *Castagna*, from Montevideo for Weymouth, MA with phosphate rock, struck the bar early today, during a blinding snowstorm and 60 mile north-west gale.

The combined life saving crews from Nauset and Cahoon's Hollow stations set up their beach gun and shot three lines across the *Castagna's* deck, but the sailors were so be-numbed by the cold that they were unable to handle the breeches buoy tackle.

The gale had moderated to 30 miles an hour, but the surf was so high that the lifesavers had to wait sometime before they could launch their lifeboat and pull out to the wreck against the wind, sea and biting cold.

Nine men, helpless from exposure to the wintery gale, were found on board. Lashed to the rigging were the bodies of captain Garva and the three men who had succumbed to the cold. The lifesavers placed the living seamen in their boat and rowed back to shore. The survivors were carried to the Marconi wireless station where medical attention was given them. All were so greatly overcome by exposure that none could give a coherent account of the disaster.

New London's "The Day" Feb. 17, 1914

Cape Cod
Shipwrecks

The Sparrow Hawk - 1626

The Cape's oldest shipwreck

The *Sparrow-Hawk* was a 'small pinnace'. She is notable as the earliest ship known from the first decades of English settlement in the New World to have survived to the present day.

She left London for the English Colonies in June 1626. Upon reaching Cape Cod, the *Sparrow-Hawk* no longer had fresh water or 'beer'. Captain Johnston was in his cabin, sick and lame with scurvy. At night, the *Sparrow-Hawk* hit a sand bar but the water was smooth and she laid out an anchor. The morning revealed that the caulking between hull planks - Oakum - had been driven out. High winds drove the *Sparrow-Hawk* over the bar and into the Harbor. Many goods were rescued and no lives were lost.

Two survivors were guided to William Bradford and the Plimouth Plantation by two Indians who spoke English. A shallop, with Governor Bradford and supplies aboard, was sent to rescue the crew.

Gov. Bradford to the rescue

Sparrow-Hawk was repaired and set to sea with cargo. However, yet another violent storm drove her onshore, and render her condition beyond repair.

Mariners and passengers went to the Plimouth Plantation. There, they were housed and fed for nine months before joining two vessels headed down the coast to Virginia. *Sparrow-Hawk* was buried in the sand and marsh mud of an Orleans, Massachusetts beach that came to be known as "Old Ship Harbor". Her 'grave' was a low oxygen environment which greatly aided preservation of hull timbers which were described as devoid of worms and barnacles. All metal fastenings had disappeared through oxidation. Her keel and hull timbers were visible from time to time when high winds shifted sand on the beach. Visitors were struck by the long "tail-like" projection from the stern. Although a single fierce storm in this area can move sand to a depth of six feet, it is judged that it took several years for the *Sparrow-Hawk* to be completely buried. Her burial site retained the name *Old Ship Harbor* into the late 19th century.

Rediscovery

In 1863, a great storm that occurred between May 4 and May 6 uncovered a great deal of the hull. It was discovered by Solomon Linnell and Alfred Rogers

Sparrow-Hawk on Display 1865

of Orleans. On May 9, Leander Crosby visited the *Sparrow-Hawk* and removed several artifacts. The rudder was few feet distant from the hull and it was removed, studied and re-assembled.

By August 1863, *Sparrow-Hawk* was once again buried beneath the surface for a few months after which she was exposed once again, and then removed above the high water mark.

Interest in the *Sparrow-Hawk* wreck was intense because it was immediately understood that this was the earliest ship wreck known from the years during which the New England Colonies were first 'planted'. Controversy immediately erupted as the hull was reconstructed. Keel, hull planks and rudder had been preserved by beach sand for more than two centuries.

Exhibitions

Sparrow-Hawk is important to the history of ship building in England and colonies in the 1600s. Several of the best naval architects of the 1860s in Boston collaborated on a reconstruction of the *Sparrow-Hawk*.

Considerable information has been gleaned from the *Sparrow Hawk* regarding hull design and construction of ships in the early 17th century.

The reconstructed *Sparrow-Hawk* hull was exhibited in several cities, including on Boston Commons in 1865, and then given to the Pilgrim Society in 1889 and exhibited for over a hundred years at the Pilgrim Hall Museum. The *Sparrow-Hawk* hull is now on long term loan from the Pilgrim Society to the Cape Cod Maritime Museum in Hyannis, Massachusetts

Sparrow-Hawk on display today

The Whydah -1717

Pirate "Black Sam Bellamy's" Ship

Just two months after Bellamy's acquisition of the *Whydah*, she and the *Mary Anne,* under the command of Consort Captain Palgrave Williams, approached Cape Cod; Williams told Bellamy that he wished to visit his family in Rhode Island. He was left at Rhode Island and his ship *Mary Anne* and its crew continued north without him. Bellamy would rejoin the *Mary Anne* at the Isle of Shoals and pick up Williams on their return trip.

The Whydah in a violent storm

Bellamy's intended reunion with his lover Maria Hallett, some believe was the reason for the early return to the Cape, was not to be.

The *Whydah* and her crew of 148 souls ran into an intense late winter storm. Despite Herculean efforts of the crew, the *Whydah* struck the bar off South Wellfleet near what is now Marconi Beach in the Cape Cod National Seashore Park and sank as raging surf tore her to pieces.

Could his lover "Goody" Hallett, who the villagers believed had become a witch, have a hand in brewing the storm that drowned her lover captain Black Bellamy and his crew. Could it be true? There are those who believe she did.

On that fateful day in April 1717, at the height of the fierce storm, she was seen high on the dunes overlooking the beach as the *Whydah* was sinking and sailors were drowning in the raging surf. People on the beach say they heard her shrieking thanks to the Devil for vengeance for Black Sam's leaving her and the death of their infant child. All this happened off the South Wellfleet dunes near the lonely dilapidated shack in which "Witch" Goody lived.

The next day a search for survivors, and perhaps treasure, revealed only bits and pieces of floating remains of the once proud flagship *Whydah* and her crew. One hundred and three bodies washed ashore and were buried by the town coroner, leaving 43 bodies unaccounted for.

Only two survived the *Wydah's* sinking to live and tell the stories of Captain Black Sam Bellamy: an Indian pilot and Thomas Davis, a Welsh carpenter. Nothing is known of what became of the pilot, but it was Davis' vivid account of the shipwreck that was passed from generation to generation to become part of Cape Cod folklore. Essentially all that is known of Black Sam the pirate comes from stories recounted by Thomas Davis. Thomas Davis was jailed, tried, and acquitted of piracy.

The bell recovered from the Whydah

The Encyclopedia Americana says of Samuel Bellamy, "*...a notorious pirate, was wrecked in his ship, the Whidah, of 23 guns and 130 men, off Wellfleet, on Cape Cod, in April 1717, after having captured several vessels on the coast and an indecisive engagement with a French ship proceeding to Quebec.*" Prior to the discovery of the ship's bell spelling its name "*Whydah*" the name of the ship was believed to be spelled "*Whidah.*" In 1984 the wreck of the "*Whydah*" was discovered by Barry Clifford of Tisbury, Massachusetts in the shallow waters off a Nat'l Seashore beach. The value of the treasure is estimated by some to approximate $500 million dollars.

Mary Anne -1717

Part of Pirate "Black Sam's" Flotilla

A few days out of Chatham, Sam Bellamy and his flotilla captured a ship carrying a significant cargo of Madeira wine.

Casks of this booty were passed freely among the sailors and a small boat was used to transport some of the wine over to the *Whydah*. Was this wine a contributing factor to the tragedy about to befall both of these vessels?

Ship going down in a storm

In the early afternoon of April 25 fog started to settle around the two vessels. The fog, in addition to the crew being drunk, defeated Bellamy's order for the *May Anne* to follow the *Whydah* and to keep close.

During the course of the evening the weather deteriorated and the pirate ships found themselves in the teeth of a full blown nor'easter. Both ships became casualties of the storm. The *Mary Anne* wrecked several miles south of the *Whydah*, leaving seven survivors. All nine survivors from the two ships were captured and prosecuted for piracy in Boston, and six were hanged in October 1717. King George's pardon of all pirates, that had been issued the previous month, arrived in Boston three weeks too late to save these pirates from the gallows.

HMS Somerset - 1778

Close to the Peaked Hill Life Saving Station lies the wreck of the British Warship *Somerset* buried beneath the sands. She was built and launched in Chatham, England, and today her

remains lay beneath the sands on a beach 30 miles east of Chatham, Massachusetts. She was built as a guard ship to the British fleet and launched July 18th, 1748. She carried sixty-four guns, and more than 500 sailors and marines.

The *HMS Somerset*

The British are Coming!

She was in Boston Harbor on the night of April 18, 1775 when a young Paul Revere and two associates rowed a skiff across the harbor to begin Revere's famous "The British are coming" ride to Lexington and Concord. He was fortunate that the men on watch aboard the *Somerset* failed to notice his movement. Several years later he wrote of the incident in a letter. . .

Two friends rowed me across the Charles River, a little to the eastward where the Somerset man-of-war lay It was then young flood, the ship was winding & the moon was rising.

Paul Revere rows past HMS Somerset

At the Battle of Bunker Hill

She was also instrumental in the outcome of the Battle of Bunker Hill. Early on the morning of June 19, 1775, the commander of the HMS *Somerset* noticed breastworks were

being constructed on Breed's Hill by the colonialists.

Being concerned of the intent of such activity he maneuvered his ship so as to command Charlestown Neck and the waters of Boston Harbor. After witnessing two failed

Don't fire until you see the whites of their eyes

attempts by British Redcoats to take the hill he ordered his marines into the ship's longboats and sent them ashore to join in the third attempt to take the hill.

The addition of the *Somerset's* marines turned the tide of battle in favor of the British's and they took what they called Bunker Hill.

Bombardment of Charlestown, Mass.

HMS Somerset took an active part in the bombardment of Charlestown as part of the Siege of Boston (April 19, 1775 – March 17, 1776) This was the opening phase of the American Revolutionary War,

Bombardment of Charlestown

The siege began on April 19 after the Battles of Lexington and Concord, when the militia from many Massachusetts communities surrounded Boston and blocked land access to the then-peninsular town, limiting British resupply to naval operations.

The Continental Congress chose to adopt the militia and form the Continental Army, and unanimously elected George Washington as its Commander in Chief. In June 1775, the British seized Bunker and Breed's Hills, but the casualties they suffered were heavy and their gains were insufficient to break the siege.

Harassed Colonial Shipping

After the Battle for Bunker Hill, the *Somerset* had returned to England but was sent back to New England in the spring 1775 primarily to harass Yankee shipping and destroy the Colonial Navy. She was quite successful in her efforts by sinking and capturing many American supply ships and privateers.

In May of 1777 the frigate *Boston* was spotted by the Somerset and she gave chase to the smaller American warship. The chase continued for several days until a powerful storm provided the *Boston's* captain the opportunity to finally elude his powerful enemy.

Ship Caught in a Gale

The End is Near

In the Fall of 1778 the British got wind of a French fleet heading towards New England. In response, the *HMS Somerset* with 550 sailors and officers aboard left her favorite harbor, Provincetown, and joined the fleet assembled to engage the French enemy

On November 1, 1778 an unusually fierce nor'easter began to lash the New England coast. The captain of HMS *Somerset* changed course to a heading that would take him back to the safety of Provincetown Harbor.

It would not be the safety of Provincetown Harbor that they reached but instead the dreaded triangle of the Highland, Pollock Rip and Chatham shoals.

The captain tried valiantly to escape the clutches of the Triangle but soon the merciless Peaked Hills Bar emerged dead ahead and the *Somerset* was soon in the grasp of the bar's sand.

A longboat was launched with fifty sailors aboard but soon capsized drowning all aboard. The tide was coming in and the captain ordered the ship's cannon thrown over the side to lighten the ship. Both of these events allowed the *Somerset* to be lifted off the bar by a huge wave and shortly pushed up onto the beach. Of the original contingent of 550 men 480 were on board when the Somerset came ashore.

The wreck was an extremely valuable commodity and people from all over the Cape descended upon Truro Beach to claim what of value they could. Brigadier Joseph Otis wrote of the mayhem wrote in a letter to the Council in Boston:

Barnstable November 4, 1778

Kind Sir
I have just received express from the Commanding Officer of the Militia of Truro, informing Me that the Somerset a British Ship is Wreckt about four miles East of the Race, and bilged, that they had got out yesterday about 60 men the Capts of the Ship and marriners included. The Sea is running high they lost one boatload of them, how many was alive aboard the wreck they could not tell.

There was some American Prisoners aboard who say they parted in the storm with 15 sail of the line bound for Boston. Have ordered an officer from here to go down and assist the officers below in conducting the prisoners along. Who shall march without delay for Boston.

But what to do for bread for them I do not know as there is none to be had where they are and their own being all wett. Any Orders from the Hon. Council if my conduct is not approved of. Please tell me by word and they shall be Pursued

I send this by express whose bill I hope will be paid which he will give in.

I am yr Honours Humble
Sevt Joseph Otis

The Council was quick to respond to Brigadier Otis but only addressed the food issue.

If you have not bread for the prisoners let them live without as many better men have done before them.

Officers Sail to Boston – Sailors Have to Walk

The officers were transported to Boston by ship leaving 450 sailors, many of them bloodied and suffering from frostbite, to walk the 130 miles or so to Boston.

Having reached Sandwich many of the outer Cape guards returned to their homes believing they had completed their duty. Many of the unguarded prisoners escaped and never re-captured.

Those prisoners that did reach Boston were placed on the French snow *Penet*. It was an old unseaworthy hulk. She wasn't an ideal choice for use as a prison ship but, was not good for much else. The conditions aboard the ship were horrendous and the prisoners suffered greatly.

HMS Somerset Cannon at Ft Independence in South Boston

Somerset Cannon now at Castle Island

Several ships were sent from Boston to bring back as much materials and goods from the wrecked *Somerset* as possible. Most of HMS *Somerset's* cannon were retrieved. In the spring of 1779 Colonel Paul Revere reported that he had mounted 21 of the cannon on platforms at Fort Independence on Castle Island in South Boston.

Reappears Out of the Sand

The remains of the *Somerset* emerged from the sands of Nauset beach in 1886 for the first time in 100 years. They reappeared again in the 1973 when thirty feet of sand was washed away by several strong storms. She reappeared again in 2008.

Land surveyors hired by the Cape Cod National Seashore created the first digital archive of the remaining visible timbers of the wreck using a three-dimensional laser scanner.

More than a dozen heavy, water-soaked ship timbers were sticking out of the sand at low tide about two miles east of the Race Point Beach ranger station in Provincetown.

The Remains of *HMS Somerset* on Truro Beach

The Gruesome Tale of a
Christmas Day Shipwreck - 1778

This is a graphic account of the Christmas Day storm in 1778 that took place in Plymouth Harbor in Massachusetts.

This story is a good representation of the horrors that have been repeated time and again in violent storms all along the shore of Cape Cod.

Wreck of the General Arnold

It was Christmas 1778, and snow was falling upon Boston Harbor. The brigantine *General Arnold*, named for the gallant hero of Quebec, was at anchor off Nantasket Road. In the early dawn, she set sail for the Carolinas, alongside the privateer *Revenge* (the *Revenge* is one of the ships lost in the Battle for New Ireland in Penobscot Bay, Maine in August of 1779).

The *Arnold* carried 21 guns, a detachment of Marines, and a cargo of military supplies for the American troops who were attempting to stop the British from cutting off the South from the Northern colonies. Her commander was Captain James Magee, an Irish born American patriot, who was looking forward to meeting up with the British, his lifelong enemy. Before the day was over, however, he would lose his ship to a greater enemy, the enraged sea.

The Brigantine General Arnold

Of the 105 men and boys who sailed with him, 81 would die a horrible death, and the others, all but himself, would be crippled for life. Under full sail, the privateers headed across Massachusetts Bay toward the open sea. The wind picked up, the snow fell harder, and soon they were in the midst of a Nor'East blizzard. Captain Barrows of the *Revenge* decided to ride out the storm in Cape Cod Bay. Magee felt that his ship could weather the storm better in Plymouth Harbor behind Gurnet Point. But, the *Arnold's* anchor wouldn't hold, and she began to drift into the long harbor.

Magee had his men dismount 16 of the deck cannons and store them below to add weight to the hull and give the vessel stability. Her sails were furled and to the topmost struck, but nothing seemed to stop the *Arnold's* dragging anchor. Huge waves broke over the bow and then quickly turned to ice.

The anchor cable broke and the *Arnold* sailed backwards into the harbor, bumped over a sand bar, and scraped to a sudden stop on top of shallow water sand flat, only a mile from shore.

At first, Magee and his men thought they could lighten the vessel and slide her over the flat to shore. With axes, they cut down her masts, but the heavy hull was already sinking into the sand, cracking her boards and leaking salt water into her hold. Icy waves washed over her main deck and the

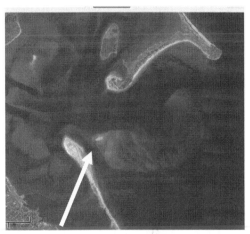

Arrow points to the resting place of the Brigantine General Arnold outside Plymouth Harbor

captain later reported "The quarter deck was the only place that could afford the most distant prospect of safety." Magee went on to say "Within a few hours, presented a scene that would shock the least delicate humanity. Some of my people were stifled to death with the snow, others perished with the extremity of the cold, and a few were washed off the deck and drowned."

There were a few bottles and casks of wine and brandy in the cargo. Some of the crew members ventured below into the half flooded hold to drown themselves in liquid warmth. Some were drunk before Captain Magee realized they had broken into the stores. He pleaded with them to pour the brandy into their shoes to prevent frostbite, instead of drinking it. Some obeyed, but those who did not were dead by the next morning.

Those huddled together on the quarterdeck, their clothes first drenched then frozen to their bodies, covered themselves with the sails for protection from the salt spray and the snow. By the morning of the 26th, thirty of them were frozen to death. The blizzard continued. Magee could see but a shadow of land through the falling snow, so he fired his signal gun in hopes of getting the attention of the people of the town. Three crewmen managed to launch the privateers long boat into the wild sea, then started rowing to shore, but they were lost sight of and never heard from again.

Late in the afternoon when there was a short break in the storm, the people of Plymouth sent dories out from shore, however, none of them could make it to the stranded vessel. They decided that the only way to the Arnold was to build a causeway of

Rescue attempt

ice and snow one mile long out to the sand flat. Working throughout the night, through the next day and night, the people of Plymouth accomplished what seemed impossible - they built a road out to the distressed privateer.

Meanwhile the shipwreck victims spent a second and third night on the quarter-deck in sub-freezing temperatures. The living feared going to sleep, knowing that if they did, they probably would not wake up again. In an attempt to block out wind and waves, they piled the dead bodies of their comrades around them. The Arnold sank deeper into the sand, knee deep water now covering the main deck. In an effort to keep his remaining crewmen and Marines alive, Captain Magee requested, then demanded, that the men keep walking around and exercising on the little deck in order to maintain their circulation.

He was especially anxious about two boys aboard: Connie Marchang, age 10 and Barney Downs, age 15. Magee prodded them to walk in place even though they were both so exhausted and frozen they could hardly stand. He urged them over and over again not to give up. Marchant later said, "I ascribe my preservation mainly to the reiterated efforts of Captain Magee."

On Monday morning, December 28th when the causeway was completed, the people of Plymouth passed over the ice to the wreck. "It was a scene unutterably awful and distressing, writes Plymouth's Doctor Thatcher. "The ship was sunk ten feet in the sand; the waves had been for about thirty six hours sweeping the main deck, and even here they were obliged to pile together dead bodies to make room for the living. Seventy dead bodies, frozen in to all imaginable postures, were strewn over the deck, or attached to shrouds and spars; about thirty exhibited signs of life, but were unconscious whether in life or death.

The fifteen year old boy Barnabas (Barney) Downs was conscious but unable to move in his frozen condition. Desperately attempting to gain attention to the fact he was yet alive, he did the only thing his frozen body was capable of: he blinked his eyes. Fortunately as a townsperson was tying a rope around the boy's waist, he saw Barney's eyes blink. Young Downs survived the ordeal but lost all of his toes and the heels of both feet to frostbite. He was alive but a cripple for the rest of his life.

The bodies remained in the posture in which they died, the features dreadfully distorted. Some were erect, some bending forward, some sitting with the head resting on the knees, and some with both arms extended, clinging to spars or some part of the vessel."

Sleds and slabs of wood were used to carry the survivors and the stiffened corpses over the ice road to shore. The dead were piled in the Plymouth Courthouse, the living brought to local homes to spend agonizing hours thawing out.

Magee skippered merchant ships out of Salem for the remainder of his life, including the famous *Astrea* that opened

41

American trade with China. Whenever in home port at Christmas, Magee called for a reunion of the 24 Arnold survivors, assisting any who were destitute with a gift from his own wages. At his request, when he died, he was buried with the Arnold crew at Burial Hill, Plymouth, MA..

Author unknown

Coincidence?

General Benedict Arnold, after whom the vessel was named, is reported to have made his decision to defect to the British on Christmas Eve 1778. The following day his namesake ship wrecks off Plymouth Harbor. Was it karma that caused the wrecking of the *General Arnold or* simply coincidence? We will never know.

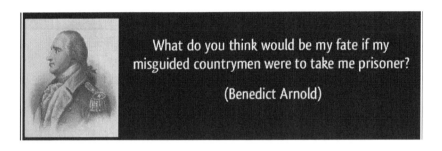

What do you think would be my fate if my misguided countrymen were to take me prisoner?

(Benedict Arnold)

It is true that by December of 1778, Arnold was growing increasingly disillusioned with American politics and the Revolution. Therefore, one might wonder that if Arnold was aware of the wreck of the privateer named after him; if so, did it occur to him it might be an omen of his impending fate.

General Arnold Burial Site

Some monuments are quite specific as to the event that occurred but often only peak ones curiosity as to the actual happenings.

Such a monument can be found on the extreme southwesterly edge of Plymouth's Famous Old Burial Hill near the Russell Street parking lot and the Old Powder House.

There is mention of seventy two seamen perishing but leaves the how and why to one's imagination.

Monument in Plymouth's Old Burial Hill to the 72 Sailors lost on the wreck of the *Benedict Arnold*

The inscriptions reads:

*In memory of Seventy two Seamen who perished
in Plymouth harbour on the 26, and 27,
days of December 1778, on board the private armed Brig, Gen.
Arnold, of twenty guns, James Magee of Boston, Commander,
sixty of whom were buried on this spot.*

On the northwesterly side: --
*Capt. James Magee died in Roxbury,
February 4, 1801; aged 51 years.*

On the southwesterly side: --
*Oh! falsely flattering were yon billows smooth
When forth, elated, sailed in evil hour,
That vessel whose disastrous fate, when told,
Fill'd every breast with sorrow and each eye
With piteous tears.*

On the southeasterly side: --
*This monument marks the resting place of
sixty of the seventy two mariners, "who perished
in their strife with the storm," and is erected by Stephen Gale
of Portland, Maine, a stranger to them, as a just memorial
of their sufferings and death.*

Dutch Frigate Erfprins -1783

303 mariners lost off Cape Cod

Few have heard of this disaster even though it involved a tragically large loss of life.

The *Erfprins* had been heavily damaged two years earlier in July of 1781 in a battle with the English fleet in the English Channel and seaworthiness was in question. Never the less, she left the Netherland, one of a convoy of four Dutch ships comprised of 3 men-of-war and a brigantine, headed for Philadelphia.

It was not long after the fleet began its way across the Atlantic that the *Erfprins* began to leak. Attempts to stop or minimize the leaking failed. Every pump available was pressed into service and crewmen pumped 24 hours a day attempting to stay or stop the leaking.

The added water made the *Erfprins* heavier and slower, holding back the progress of the entire fleet. The fleet commander

The Dutch Battleship *Erfpins* with 54 guns and a crew of 343

decided that each ship should be on its own. Soon the leaking battleship was all alone in the middle of the vast and unpredictable Atlantic.

On September 19 the weeks of fair weather that they had been enjoying changed and now they found themselves in the teeth of a violent storm. Both the main mast and the mizzenmast came crashing down onto the deck severely injuring several seamen.

The storm created terrific damage to the ship; men were feverishly pumping out the seawater that now was coming in from the leaking seams as well as from the waves crashing on the deck. The *Erfprins* sank even deeper into the sea.

De-Masted and Adrift

The storm broke that night and the following day the crew made as many repairs as they could and jury rigged a mast of sorts. Because of their condition they were now essentially alone and adrift in the vast ocean and slowly sinking.

Pumping continued 24/7 but it became clear it was a hopeless task. They had been drifting for nine weeks and still no sight of land. Food was all but gone and drinking water fouled and not fit to drink. The situation was bad and no rescue ships were ever sighted.

They had drifted/sailed into the Gulf Stream. It was the Gulf Stream which flows north along the Atlantic coast from Florida to the Maritimes that brought them off the shores of Cape Cod.

On November 25, 1783 the ship had wallowed its way to where they could see land. It was Cape Cod.

Ship slipping beneath the waves

It appeared they had reached land just in time as the *Erfprins* was sinking ever more deeply despite the constant efforts of those manning her pumps.

The captain launched the ship's longboat and he and thirty nine handpicked men pulled away from the ship and headed for the shore of the Cape. Survivors aboard the longboat estimate that the *Erfprins* sank three minutes later carrying 303 sailors to their watery grave.

The longboat hailed, and was rescued by an outbound sailing vessel which then transferred the survivors to a fishing boat headed to Gloucester. It is here that the story ends.

Almira – 1827

A tragedy close to shore and home

The winter of 1827 was unusually cold, one of the coldest on record. It was cold enough to cause many ships much hardship as ice froze on the ship's masts and rigging. Several ships ran aground on the rocks and beaches all along the Massachusetts coast.

The cold was so intense that some sailors froze to death and others lost hands and feet to frostbite. It was against this

Schooner in a Gale

backdrop that a small schooner, laden with wood, left Sandwich Harbor. The harsh weather had abated and the *Almira* headed north on her fateful journey. The captain was sure that, now with a southerly wind and warmer temperatures, a few days of moderate weather lay ahead.

It is reported that, as she left the harbor, an old and experienced coaster captain remarked - "Gone out! he will never come in again!" The captain of the *Almira* was Josiah Ellis, along with his son and a sailor named John Smith, sailed north and obviously was unaware of this ominous prediction.

46

The wind became variable and progress was slowed so that by evening the ship was only off Manomet's Mary Ann Rocks. Darkness was approaching and temperatures falling to historic lows. The captain, knowing that he must make harbor soon lest they freeze, set his course to nearby Plymouth Harbor.

The winds shifted and increased from the north. Reaching the safety of Plymouth's Harbor meant tacking into this gale. The captain knew this was next to impossible given the narrow channel with rocks on one side and a sandbar on the other so he changed course and headed back to Sandwich.

No sooner had they changed course but the wind and accumulating ice broke the mainsail and it came crashing down onto the deck. The frozen sea spray now coated everything and made clearing the debris on the deck or trimming the jib impossible. The violent wind and accumulated ice tore the jib's canvass to shreds.

Almira was now out of control and at the mercy of the storm. The frozen sailors were unable to maneuver their vessel.

The ship had drifted through the coldest night of memory. Ocean spray froze on contact with everything it touched. The smallest line became as large as a hawser. The crumpled pile of sail and mast on the deck filled with a heavy mass of ice. The *Almira* was becoming so top heavy that her capsizing was becoming increasingly more imminent.

The fierce wind blew them helplessly down the coast past Sandwich, Barnstable and Yarmouth to where their fateful journey would soon end on a rocky ledge off Dennis. They could see the lights in the windows and smoke from coming from the chimneys of the homes on the nearby shore. So close to safety and home but yet – so very far.

Dennis residents could see the approaching schooner and wondered if anyone was aboard. Soon three men became visible standing on the ice covered deck as statues. They were crusted in ice.

As rescuers raced to the beach *Almira* was caught up by a huge wave and crashed down on the rocky ledge. The three ice covered sailors, having been aboard the ship throughout the night in below zero temperatures, were weak, close to death and expecting their ship to go to pieces any moment.

A boat was launched into sea which was like slush close to shore, and out towards the ship but a large wave swamped it. A line thrown from the shore prevented the rescuers from becoming casualties. Meanwhile John Smith sat down on the windlass and died. Helplessly the rescuers on the shore saw the captain fall to the deck and watched him too die.

The tide had been coming in and a huge wave lifted the *Almira* from the rocky ledge and threw it up on the beach. Young Ellis was saved. Captain Ellis' body was retrieved but Smith's body was washed away. When the rescuers climbed on board they found young Ellis with his hands frozen to the ropes and his feet and ankles encrusted with ice. Despite the best medical attention available, he eventually lost both hands and both feet to frostbite.

The Josephus – 1849

It was at the height of a furious a northeasterly gale in April of 1849 that the British Schooner Josephus went aground off Highland Light. She was heavily laden with iron rails. Perhaps her cargo was part of the reason that she went to pieces so quickly.

A crowd quickly gathered on the beach as word spread of the event. Efforts were begun to save the men who could be seen and their frantic cries for help heard above the crashing surf.

The sailors could be seen frantically clinging to the masts and riggings as they tried to avoid being washed into the raging foam. The onlookers did not dare launch into the mountainous surf fearing for their own lives.

Word had reached two fishermen who, having themselves escaped the storm returning from a fishing trip, rushed to the beach to render such aid as they might. They spotted a dory, and headed to the surf to launched and make their way toward the stricken vessel. They were warned by onlookers of the danger but are said to have responded – *"We cannot stand it longer to see these poor fellows being swept into the sea. We are going to reach them."*

They had gone no more than thirty yards when a giant wave broke into their dory engulfing them in the foaming surf. They were never seen again, dead or alive.

Night began to fall but the storm raged on. The cries from the stricken sailors became weaker and weaker and sometime after dark, the cries were no more – the crowd on the beach went home to their warm beds.

It was about midnight when the lighthouse keeper, not being able to sleep, went for a walk along the beach and heard a moan. It was coming from some wreckage floating in the water. He rushed out and found a semi conscious sailor. The only survivor – 23 of his shipmates and the two heroic rescuers had perished.

The Franklin – 1849

Planned shipwreck claims the life of the plotter

Headlines of the Boston Courier, March 3, 1849 declare the Loss of the sailing ship Franklin and the lives of eleven, including that of the captain.

The paper's article reads:

> *Mr. Hopkins of Wellfleet arrived in this city last night and states that the ship Franklin, Capt. Smith from London, of and for Boston, went ashore at Wellfleet, Cape Cod, on Thursday morning at nine o'clock, and Captain Smith with the first mate, and eight others, perished. The ship went to pieces and her cargo was scattered along the shore.*

Thus began a story that would expand beyond just the shipwreck and involve one of America's most famous authors.

The *Franklin* was en route from Deal, England, to Boston, with passengers and cargo when she foundered near Newcomb's Hollow, on the ocean side of Wellfleet.

The morning the *Franklin* went down Captain Isaiah Hatch of Wellfleet was out roaming the beach. As wreckage came drifting ashore he fished out a valise, which proved to be Capt. Smith's.

The valise contained correspondence between the owners, James W. Wilson and John W. Crafts of Boston, and Capt. Smith unmistakably revealing that the trio had insured the *Franklin* for twice her real value, and conspired to sink the ship and split the insurance money.

Meanwhile a good part of the *Franklin's* cargo had been salvaged by the people of Wellfleet and other Cape Cod towns. Among the items saved from the sea was a choice selection of nursery stock, bought in England and Scotland by a South Boston man named Bell, with the idea of setting up a horticultural business in this country.

Henry David Thoreau visited the Cape the following year and was introduced to an eye witness to the *Franklin* tragedy, a Mr. Jack Newcomb a/k/a the "Wellfleet Oysterman." Thoreau recounts Newcomb's story. . .

He told us the story of the Franklin, which took place the previous spring; how a boy came to his house early in the morning to know whose boat it was upon the shore, for there was a vessel in distress, and he, being an old man, first ate his breakfast, and then walked over to the top of the hill by the shore, and sat down there, having found a comfortable seat, and sat down there to see the ship wrecked. She was on the bar only a quarter mile from him, and still nearer to the men on the beach, who had got a boat ready. . .

Casualty of the sea

"I saw the captain get on his boat," said he "he had one little one, and then they jumped into it one after another, down as straight as an arrow. I counted them. There were nine. One was a woman, and she jumped as straight as any one of them. The sea took them back, one wave over them, and when they came up there were six still clinging to the boat; I counted them. The next wave turned the boat bottom upward, and emptied them all out. None of them ever came ashore alive."

When rescuers finally reached the *Franklin* they were able to rescue all of the passengers except for one woman who had been washed overboard earlier. Of the thirty one passengers aboard the Franklin, twenty were saved while eleven including its dishonest captain perished.

The Caledonia – 1862

New Years Eve tragedy

It was December 31, 1862 during a storm that raged the entire Atlantic sea coast. The British steamer *Caledonia* was headed for New York when she ran aground on the Cape's infamous Peaked Hill Bar off Highland Lighthouse.

The ship quickly broke in half and a total loss but her cargo of iron rails was salvaged later. The tug *Walpole* arrived on the scene and removed the captain and his crew safely onto his ship. Captain Weston of the *Caledonia* admitted later that he had mistaken the Highland Light flash for that of Race Point Lighthouse and had set his course accordingly.

Same storm claims USS Monitor

It was during this same storm that the *USS Monitor* sank while rounding Cape Hatteras.

It is reported:

> *As the Monitor prepared to round Cape Hatteras, waves hit the turret so hard it trembled. But the crew was elated: "Hurrah for the first iron-clad that ever rounded Cape Hatteras!" they cried. "Hurrah for the little boat that is first in everything!" By 7:30 p.m. one of the hawsers snapped and the Monitor began rolling wildly.*

Four hours later the *USS Monitor* would sink taking thirty three sailors with her.

USS Monitor sinks while being towed by
USS Rhode Island

The Peruvian – 1873

T'was the night after Christmas

Captain Charles H Hannah had returned from a long but successful journey from Calcutta to New York with a cargo of tin and sugar and now was anxious to head north to New Hampshire and his lovely sweetheart.

All had gone well until the *Peruvian* sailed into the teeth of what later would be called the "Christmas Gale of 1873". The weather closed in and the fog made visual navigation impossible. Capt. Hannah was not concerned as he had set a northerly course designed to take his ship to the east of Cape Cod and onto New Hampshire.

Unfortunately, his calculations were off by a few miles and the *Peruvian* ran aground upon the unforgiving and dreaded Peaked Hill Shoal off Highland Light and Chatham. The ship quickly broke to pieces and all hands perished in the foaming surf.

Ship and sailors in distress

Twenty eight sailors perished with only three bodies ever recovered. The captain's was not one of them.

Several days later word of the disaster reached his intended in New Hampshire – the man she loved had been carried to his death on the night after Christmas.

The Francis – 1873

Another casualty of the Christmas Gale of 1873

The iron bark *Francis* came ashore 175 yards off the beach at Truro. Onlookers watched helplessly from the beach as huge waves relentlessly crashed into the vessel.

The closest rescue boat was a double ended whaleboat located on the Bay side of the Cape several miles away. It took twenty men to drag the boat to the Truro beach. Deep snow, gale force winds and freezing temperatures impeded their progress but they urgently pressed on. They finally reached the shore where they quickly launched the precious craft into the surf.

Upon reaching the stricken Francis, they found its captain in his bunk as he had taken ill several days before. He and all of the twenty crewmen were

Ship aground in a storm

safely brought to shore. However, the captain died a few days later.

After a few days, salvage of the ship and its cargo of sugar began. Once in awhile, as the sugar was being hoisted from the hold, a bale would break. The supervising foreman authorized the twenty five men on the salvage crew to scoop up the fallen sugar and bring it home in their lunch buckets.

This generous practice came to an end when the boat carrying the twenty five workers to shore nearly capsized because of the extra weight the forty or more pounds of sugar each worker was carrying in his "lunch pail".

The Giovanni – 1875

All aboard perish save one

The Italian Bark *Giovanni* left Palermo, Italy bound for America with a cargo of nuts, sumac and brimstone. On March 4th she ran into a gale off of Cape Cod. The Nor'easter drove her onto Peaked Hill Shoal off Highland Light three miles from the Highland Life-Saving station.

The mountainous surf made firing the mortar gun and then rigging breeches bouy from the ship to the beach the preferred method of rescue. The rescue gun was fired but time and again the terrific gale prevented the shot from reaching the stricken craft.

Sailors grasping hold of debris

The *Giovanni* was breaking up and debris began floating ashore when two sailors aboard the ship jumped into the sea in an attempt to reach safety. The cannon shots were aborted and all hands rushed to the water's edge in an attempt to reach the sailors.

One of the two jumpers had disappeared from view but the other was floating ashore with the surf. The rescuers wadded into the raging sea joining hands forming a human chain. Fortune was with them and the Italian sailor was grabbed by the foremost rescuer and pulled to shore. Of the fifteen Italian sailors aboard the *Giovanni* he was the only one to survive.

The storm raged through the night and rescuers kept watch hoping for an opportunity to save more of the *Giovanni's* crew. When dawn broke three men were seen moving on *Giovanni's* deck. Soon the ship broke asunder and the three sailors were tossed into the sea where they were able to grab onto some floating debris.

The long encounter had drained these sailors of their strength and half way to the shore they simultaneously slipped from their floatation and sank beneath the waves.

Five Wrecks off Orleans
January 3, 1878

Blizzard Conditions Claim 5 Ships

The seas were extremely rough and it was snowing a thick heavy snow driven by gale force winds from the northeast. The flood tide, violent gale, soft sand and four inches of wet snow hampered rescue efforts. Hauling the wagons and handcarts loaded with mortar, ropes, pulleys and breeches bouys was made even more difficult by the snow clogging the wagon wheels pausing progress to beat off the snow.

The flood tide made travel along the beach impossible is some of the rescue attempts that day. Rescuers were forced off the beach, as seas were crashing into the cliff-side, and across the top of the bluffs in order to make way to the wrecks.

Schooner *J. G. Babcock* – Jan, 1878

Seven Lives Were Claimed

The schooner *J. G. Babcock* out of Hoboken on way to Boston was spotted hard on the beach at seven in the morning by a lifesaver from Station No. 11 (Orleans) on his morning patrol. The wreck lay two miles north of the station. The lifesavers immediately left the warmth of the station and made way to the stricken vessel.

In addition to the stormy conditions, travel to the stricken vessel was made even more difficult as one crew member was missing being out on patrol to the south of the station.

Within ninety minutes they were abreast of the wreck and came upon a small boat, apparently from the vessel, with an oar lashed to it. Nearby was the top of a chest. The vessel was within 300 yards of the beach yet the heavy snow prevented her from being seen. Fortunately, they got a glimpse of her only few minutes after they passed the small boat.

She only became visible when the squalls abated momentarily revealing only her torn sails – the blizzard quickly shrouded her again from view. When the storm next allowed a view they witnessed her masts fall. Next they saw were pieces of the ship washing up on the shore. She had split in half lengthwise and broken off at the floor timbers.

It is surmised, based upon the boat and chest on the beach, that the seven man crew had attempted to row ashore but were upset in the surf and drowned. Four sailors washed ashore over the next two days, the other three were never recovered

Sea Lion – Jan, 1878

All Hands Survive

The *Sea Lion*, bound from Hoboken, NJ, to St John, New Brunswick was to be found stranded within 200 yards of Orleans Beach. This ship had come ashore just a half mile from the *J. G. Babcock* and was spotted by the station crew there. As the *Babcock* was past assistance the lifesavers hurried on to assist the *Sea Lion*.

When they arrived abreast of her they found her capsized boat up on the shore, but not a trace of her crew. Believing the crew had perished while attempting to reach the shore, they began a search of the beach looking for survivors or bodies. It was then that they got word that the crew was safe and sound back at the Lifesaving Station.

After the storm

According to the ship's captain, his ship struck at 6:30 a.m. and he immediately let go his anchor to bring her head round to the sea that he might lower his boat for the shore. He was not aware there was a lifesaving station on the coast, or he would have remained with his crew aboard until help arrived, as he thought upon leaving the vessel that there was little possibility of reaching the shore alive.

That he and his four men succeeded in reaching the beach during the raging blizzard is miraculous. There was not but one chance in ten of success, the boat had almost filled with water, one more crashing wave would have surely thrown them all to their demise in the icy Atlantic waters.

Once upon the beach the shipwrecked sailors now had to contend with the fierce winter blizzard on the shore. They soon made their way behind the sand hills and somewhat out of the teeth of the storm. At the same time the lifesaving crew was making their way to the stranded ship along the beach. In this way they would unknowingly pass each other.

The sailors came upon the Lifesaving Station, which was locked because the occupants were at the wreck, gained entrance through a window.

All were frost bitten and the captain had severely damaged shoulder aboard his ship. After two days of rehabilitation, the sailors boarded an Old Colony Railroad car, tickets courtesy of the Lifesaving crew, and headed for Boston and the British consul.

Triple Wreck off Pamet River Lifesaving Station - Jan. 3, 1878

Schooners *Pow-Wow*, *Addie P. Avery*, and *Miles Standish*

It was a fierce January blizzard that wreaked havoc along the Cape Cod shore that fateful January day. About 4:30 in the morning a patrol-man awakened the crew at Pamet River Lifesaving Station #8 with the news that a three masted schooner was ashore upon the outer bar a half mile north of the station.

It was the *Addie P. Avery*, of Port Jefferson, Long Island. The station crew leapt into action and was engaged in preparations for a rescue when a second patrolman scurried into the station with news of yet another ship in distress. It was the *Pow-Wow*, a fishing schooner, of Provincetown, ashore about one third mile south of the station.

The station's Captain was faced with a dilemma. Two ships, in opposite directions from his station, needed his help but he could only assist one at a time. If he divided his force of six to attempt a rescue of both ships, none would be saved. Three men could not do the job and the blinding blizzard conditions prevented his calling for assistance from neighboring stations.

The Captain choose to assist the *Pow-Wow* first reasoning that because of her position she was less likely to survive the sea's pounding for very long and was more likely to have more men on board.

The mountainous surf conditions made use of a surfboat for rescue impossible so the mortar and breeches bouy rescue method was prepared for the rescue. The needed apparatus was hauled laboriously through the soft and wet slushy snow by hand cart to a position abreast of the *Pow-Wow*. A second trip was needed to bring the rest of the required apparatus so a portion of the crew was sent back to the station while the remaining crew members prepared for the rescue.

What! Another Ship!

Dawn was breaking when suddenly, through a rift in the whirling snow; another schooner was spotted about a mile further southward. It turned out it to be the *Miles Standish*, also of Provincetown. The Captain left his crew in charge of his second in command and hurried to the stricken vessel. As he came close he saw members of the ship's crew leaping into the surf to reach shore.

Fortunately for the crew, the ship's commander, when she first struck the outer bar, had hoisted on all the sail he could thereby forcing the ship over the bar and up onto the beach where the entire crew reached shore safely.

The Lifesaving Station Captain's arrival was fortunate for the ship's crew was soaked through to their skins and, in the icy winter blast, would have certainly perished from exposure while they wandered the beach seeking shelter. The station Captain guided the survivors to the Lifesaving Station using a path behind the beach hills where they were less exposed to the bitter gale. After reaching the station and providing them dry clothing and nourishment the station's Captain returned to his crew who were assisting the *Pow-Wow*.

Upon arriving back at the Pow-Wow he found his crew was delayed in deploying the lifesaving apparatus as the ship was dragging anchor along the outer bar. Soon she fetched up on her small anchor and the lifesavers fired their mortar. The first shot fell high in the rigging across her main-topmast stay.

The ship's crew, who were hanging on in the fore-rigging and on the bowsprit, were all half frozen and benumbed. They needed all the strength they had left in them just to hold on as the ship was rolling heavily and so no-one made an effort to go aloft and reach it. After an ineffectual attempt to get the line within reach by working it from shore the decision was made to fire a second shot.

This time the aim was lowered so as to carry the shot and line amongst the men. The shot was successful, the line falling upon the bow-sprit, where it was grasped by the sailors clinging there. Soon they had on board the inch and a half whip-line attached but the wreck was again drifting southward. Erecting the breeches bouy or the life-car was now out of the question; moreover, the wreck was now beginning to break up in the surf.

The lifesavers made signs to the sailors that they should attach themselves to the line and jump overboard. Ten, of the vessel's fifteen person company, were saved in this way, one

Schooner breaking up in the surf

by one drawn ashore. This desperate measure, which necessity compelled, was made even more dangerous by the terrible surf and the presence of fragments of the ship as she broke up. Timbers, spars and planking from the vessel, capable of inflicting fatal wounds, broken bones and serious bruises were awash in the surf and the seamen's path to shore. Worse still were the masses of tangled and writhing cordage in the surf ready to snare anyone struggling through the breakers.

As the sailors leapt from the ship into the surf, station men, with cords around their waists, the ends of which were held by their fellows, would go deep into the treacherous undertow to aid them. At one point, the sailors on the bow-sprit had not hauled back sufficient line to allow the next passenger to be pulled ashore. Realizing that they were about to lose their only chance for life, they secured the line onboard. This caused the sailor on the line to be held fast in the breakers.

To save him, two surfmen, at great risk to themselves, rushed into the surf and with herculean efforts succeeded in taking him out off the line in which he had fastened himself, and brought him ashore.

In the instance of the tenth sailor saved, the sailor attached to the line had gotten caught in the wreckage of the jib, and two of the surfmen who had gone into the breakers to clear him themselves became entangled with him in the snarl of floating cordage and now all three were in extreme danger. A third surfman rushed into the boiling surf and with his knife cut them free by severing the line to the ship.

This daring feat, necessary for the safety of the three men, resulted in the sacrifice of the connection thus far maintained with the vessel. One sailor remained on board, apparently senseless, either frozen or clinging to the rigging. The vessel had now drifted close enough to shore that a line could be thrown aboard using a heaving stick. The sole remaining sailor made no effort to grasp it and soon fell, lifeless into the sea. A surfman plunged into the undertow to retrieve him but to no avail. He was lost.

Another sailor had previously dropped from the bow-sprit exhausted, and had perished, and a boy had frozen to death. These three lives were all that were lost after the arrival of the lifesaving crew upon the scene. It appears that when the vessel first struck, the captain and one man fell overboard and were drowned. Five sailors in all perished. The remaining ten were saved by the strenuous and heroic actions of the life-saving crew.

What about the *Addie P. Avery*?

During the operations for the rescue of the *Pow-Wow*, the quantity of wreckage, including her bow, indicated that the *Addie P. Avery* had broken up soon after striking. There were six persons on board, all of whom were lost. The twenty two sailors saved from the *Miles Standish* and the *Pow-Wow* were sheltered at the station until the storm subsided. All were provided with clothing and free passage by rail to their homes by the station crew.

The Trumbull – 1880

The sloop *Trumbull* was spotted hard aground on Peaked Hill Bar. The patrol from the Peaked Hill Life-Saving station spotted the wreck while on patrol just south of the station.

She had left Rockport November 29 with a crew of five and a cargo of granite. She was headed for New York when she ran aground early in the morning of the next day.

Captain David Atkins was the person in charge of the life-station and it was he, along with six men, who launched their life-saving boat into the surf and rowed to the stranded craft.

Upon arriving at the *Trumbull* Capt. Atkins determined it was too dangerous to approach the ship any closer and ordered the crew to jump into the water where they could be pulled up onto the life-boat. Three sailors complied and were immediately pulled to safety of the surf-boat and then to the shore. The captain and the first mate of the *Trumbull* refused to leave their ship, deciding instead to remain on board the stranded craft.

Captain Atkins was very troubled by their decision and shortly after depositing the three crewmen safely on shore, he headed back out to the ship in a second attempt to rescue the remaining mariners.

When they reached the ship things turned bad. As the life-boat approached the *Trumbull* the boom and main sheet of the *Trumbull* came crashing down capsizing the rescue craft and plunging the rescuers into the water. Captain Atkins was drowned.

The tide was rising and before too long the *Trumbull* was freed of the bar and floated off to continue her voyage while the rescuer, Captain David Atkins, lay in his watery grave.

Yacht, Mystery - Aug 1883

Searching for the *Mystery*

PROBABLE LOSS OF A YACHT AND ALL ON BOARD.

Mr. George H. Sargent, of the firm of Sargent & Co., at No. 37 Chambers-street, left New-Haven, Conn., yesterday, in a steam launch to cruise along the Connecticut and Massachusetts coast, making a thorough search for any trace of the missing sloop-yacht *Mystery*. He was accompanied by a volunteer crew of friends. The *Mystery* left New-Haven Aug. 10 for Nantucket, expecting to make the run in three days. Her passengers were Leicester Sergent, of New-Haven, and Rupert Sergent, of this City, sons of George H. Sergent, of this City; Robert H. Hawkins, of the New-Haven Ruffle Company, and a Mr. Bartlett, of this City, whose Christian name is not known at the office of Sergeant & Co., of this City. The young men were all between 20 and 26 years of age, and were expert yachtsmen and swimmers. Nothing had yet been heard

Sailing Yacht in Rough Seas

of the *Mystery* of her crew, all of whom it is feared went down with her during one of the severe storms which prevailed about that time.

The missing *Mystery* is a sloop-rigged centre-board yacht, 26 feet 6 inches in length over all, 11 feet in breadth, 3 feet 6 inches deep, and with a draught of 3 feet. She was built by J. B. Herreshoff, of Bristol, R. I., and was owned by F. H. Baldwin, of New-Haven. She belonged to the New-Haven Yacht Club's fleet, and was one of its fastest vessels.

The New York Times, New York, NY 23 Aug 1883

THE VICTIMS OF THE *MYSTERY*

MR. ROBERT H. HAWKINS'S BODY REACHES THIS CITY.

The body of Mr. Robert H. Hawkins, one of the passengers on the yacht *Mystery,* which went down with all on board in Buzzard's Bay, arrived in this City yesterday and was taken to a Brooklyn undertaker's establishment, where it will remain until removed to Yaphank, Long Island, for burial early next week. It was closed in a hermetically sealed casket.

The body was accidentally found on a little island off Pocasset, in Buzzard's Bay, by a farmer named Jesse Barlow, who was out huckle-berrying. It was imbedded in the long sea-grass which grows in profusion all

Cape Cod Sea Grass

about that vicinity. Mr. Barlow knew nothing of the loss of the *Mystery* or of the reward offered for the recovery of young Hawkins's body until he was notified by the Selectman of Pocasset, to whom he reported his discovery. the old man seemed perfectly bewildered when Mr. Burlinger's representative gave him the $100 reward, as he had probably never had so much money at any one time in his life.

The possession of the money made him the lion of the town for a time. No traces of the bodies of Messrs. Leicester Sargent or Joseph P. Bartlett have yet been discovered and fears are entertained that the bodies will not be discovered. The body of Mr. Rupert Sargent will probably be interred in New-Haven, Conn.

The New York Times, New York, NY

The Mystery is Found

BOSTON, Mass., Aug. 25. ---A New-Bedford dispatch says:
"The yacht *Mystery*, recently lost and towed to this port, was
hauled upon the beach at Crow Island this afternoon at low
water and examined. Her bottom is in good condition with the
exception of a small hole on her port quarter, just above the
water-line, which was probably done in towing her to port or
else stove while in the water after filling. The personal effects
of the Sargent brothers were found as well as the charts, &c.
One life preserver was also found, showing that but three had
been made use of. A calendar clock in the cabin had stopped
at 6:44 with the indicator at 12, showing that the disaster
occurred on the 12th inst. Something startling must have
happened, for, when found, she had all sail set, jib and flying
jib, and the tender to beach her. The most plausible theory is
that she capsized, as no mark of her going on rock appears.

The vessel is over-sparred and carried too much sail. No other
body has yet been found, though the shores have been
patrolled continually. The body of Rupert Sargent will be
taken to New-York for interment."

The New York Times, New York, NY

The Loss of the *Mystery*

NEW-BEDFORD, Mass., Aug. 26.----The friends of Leicester
Sargent and Joseph W. Bartlett, the missing men of the yacht
Mystery's party, are still here making every possible effort to
find the bodies. It is the opinion of those best informed that
unless the bodies are found in a day or two, they will not be
recovered.

The New York Times, New York, NY

SUPPOSED TO BE MR. BARTLETT'S BODY.

BOSTON, Sept. 17. ----A body which was washed ashore on Sunday at West Falmouth is now supposed to be that of Joseph W. Bartlett, of New-York, who was lost from the yacht *Mystery* on Aug. 12.

The New York Times, New York, NY 18 Sept 1883

PROBABLY NOT MR. BARTLETT'S BODY.

NEW-HAVEN, Sept. 18.---A dispatch was published in several newspapers to-day stating that a body washed ashore last Sunday at West Falmouth, Mass., is supposed to be that of Joseph W. Bartlett, of New-York, who was lost from the yacht *Mystery* on Aug. 12. The yacht left this city for an eastern cruise on Aug. 10, those on board being Leicester Sargent and his brother Rupert, Robert H. Hawkins and Mr. Bartlett. The bodies of Mr. Hawkins and Rupert Sargent were recovered, and now, if the supposition in to-days dispatch should turn out to be true, the body of another of the unfortunate quartet has been washed ashore at about the same place where the boat went down, and the other two bodies were found. A. W. Parmelee, with Sargent & Co., of this city, told a reporter to-day, however, that he had doubts about the body being that of Mr. Bartlett, for the reason that in such an event agents engaged by Mr. Parmelee at West Falmouth would have certainly telegraphed on Sunday or yesterday to this city. Mr. Parmelee added that he had this morning received a letter dated yesterday from Mrs. Bartlett at Boston, and she had received no news of her son.

The New York Times, New York, NY 19 Sept 1883

Steamers TWILIGHT & JOHN BROOKS Collide, - 1884

7 Excursion Boats and a Tug Participate in it.

BOSTON, Mass., Aug. 20.--The most complicated collision ever known in Massachusetts waters occurred at 5 P. M. yesterday. Seven excursion boats and a tug participating.

A dense fog prevailed. At 5 o'clock the Portland steamer *John Brooks* with 80 passengers, when off Buoy 8, sighted the big Nantucket steamer *Twilight* with 500 passengers. Both boats stopped, but too late. The *Brooks* crashed into the *Twilight* and a panic at once ensued. Four *Twilight* passengers jumped on the *Brooks* thinking their own boat was sinking. In swinging away from the *Twilight*, the *Brooks* narrowly escaped collision with the Portland steamer *Penobscot* and the harbor steamer *Gov. Andrew*. Clearing these she struck the *Rose Standish*, scraping her entire side and crating another panic. Clearing the *Standish*, the *Brooks* nearly ran down the propeller *Baltimore,* but succeeded in getting to her wharf without further damage. The *Twilight* started for Hull and a few moments afterwards struck the Plymouth excursion steamer *Stamford* with 250 passengers, scraping her from bow to stern and taking off nearly the whole side to the water's edge. The paddle wheel was crushed and the shafts were broken, leaving her helpless. Her passengers thought she was sinking and were with difficulty kept from leaping into the water. The *Twilight* offered no aid but kept right on. A tug towed the *Stamford* to her wharf. The only person injured was an unknown lady from Somerville, who was in the stateroom on that side of the Stamford which was struck. She was taken home unconscious. A negro on the *Stamford* was knocked into the water but was rescued. The *Twilight* now lies at Hull, unable to get to Boston. The *Empire State* was reported wrecked, but lies anchored in Nantasket roads, waiting for tide. The *Brooks, Twilight* and *Stamford* are badly damaged, and will be laid up several days.

Matilda Buck – 1890

British Bark

On January 9, 1890 Matilda Buck, an English brig went ashore and wrecked on the southwest end of Long Point , Provincetown south of Wood End light.

British Bark Matilda Buck

Messenger – Circa 1890

A Total Wreck

Kattie J. Barrett – 1890

Ran aground on Nauset Beach February 24, 1890

This 191' four masted schooner was built in 1887, at Bath, Maine. She was carrying a cargo of ice when it struck the bars

Salvaging of the Kattie J. Barrett underway

a quarter mile off Nauset Beach.

Crews from the Orleans and Nauset Life Saving stations rescued the nine sailors aboard. She was severely damaged and almost a total loss when she stranded.

After seven months of being pounded by the seas, the *Katie J. Barrett* was sold, hauled off and towed to Boston to be repaired and renamed Star of the Sea. She was finally lost on October 26, 1911 by stranding on Florida Reefs.

The Jason – 1892

A ship cursed with bad luck

The fateful voyage began on a voyage in February, 1891 from England to Zanzibar with a load of coal. Three days later she was rammed by the steamer *Trilawie* from Cornwall. The *Jason* survived this incident and was repaired in dry dock and her fateful voyage continued.

The ship ran into a terrific gale while rounding Cape of Good Hope. One of the sailors lost his grip while in the rigging and fell to his death on the deck below.

She reached Zanzibar without further incident, unloaded the coal and continued on to Calcutta where a crewman was drowned when he fell into the harbor.

The *Jason* was loaded with a large cargo of jute and began its fateful journey to Boston and immediately ran into a great hurricane. After battling the storm for three days the Jason was in ruin. Her masts had been broken off and washed away by the storm and her captain had broken his leg.

They rigged a jury mast and limped into the harbor at Mauritius Island, several hundred miles east of Zanzibar. It took an entire six months to repair the

Winslow Homer's last painting depicts a De-masted ship in a storm

Jason. Everything, except her hull, had to be replaced.

They began the journey to Boston anew, now with a different captain as the captain with his broken leg had been returned to England. Bad luck continues as they had not been out of port a day when another sailor fell from the rigging and was killed.

A few days later the ship had to return to port because the cargo of jute was swelling so much that it threatened to crack the ship's hull.

The journey to New England continued without further incident until in December of 1893, almost two years after leaving England, the Jason was off Cape Cod's coast in a dense fog.

Surfboat heads to the *Jason* after the storm

The captain had set a course that he thought would bring him to Boston.   Unfortunately, he ended up in the dreaded Peaked Hills Bar Triangle off Chatham and Highland lights. Once inside the Triangle, escape was impossible with an easterly blow as the narrow strip of water between Pollock Rip Shoal and the beach made maneuvering to safety impossible. Running aground was inevitable and, with a heavy wind and surf, deadly.

The nor'easter had the ship firmly in her grasp and the rain turned to sleet and snow. Ice began to form on the decks and rigging. The heavy seas and icing of the ship prevented her longboat from being launched.

Meanwhile, on shore possible rescuers watched helplessly as the doomed ship made her way down the coast past one life saving station after another until she finally ran hard aground near the Parnet River Life Saving Station off Truro's Ballston Beach.

Bales of jute and wreckage from the ship littered the beaches for miles. Jute was a valuable commodity used in the making of rope critical for use by sailing vessels and a ready customer was the nearby Plymouth Cordage Co.

Lifesavers were unable to launch into the surf and fired their gun to the vessel. There was no response for all but one of the sailors were killed when mizzenmast when it crashed onto the sea. It was the practice for seamen to lash themselves to a mast or rigging during a violent storm to prevent being washed overboard by the crashing waves.

Samuel Evans, Sole survivor of the Jason wreck

One young sailor, Samuel Evans, was able to free himself from the mast and, because he had on a life vest, was washed ashore exhausted but able to grab onto a bale of jute to prevent the undertow from washing him back to the sea.

When help reached him he was semi-conscious but able to ask; "Be I saved?" The answer was Yes! But he was the only one to survive.

Twenty six of his crew mates perished and he was the only one left to tell the tale of the unlucky ship *Jason*.

Samuel Evans returned to England and resumed his sailing career but, on his first cruise it is reported that he fell out of his bunk, broke his neck, and died.

Nineteen of the twenty six victims were recovered from the sea and are buried in Wellfleet Cemetery, seven were never found and three were buried elsewhere.

Jason Shipwreck Monument 1893

IN MEMORY OF
THOSE BRAVE MARINERS LOST IN THE WRECK
OF THE BRITISH SHIP *JASON* OFF THE BACK
SHORE OF CAPE COD DECEMBER 5, 1893

GEORGE MILLAN, CAPTAIN
ARCHIBALD GALBREATH
PETER BLACK
JOSEPH F OWEN
ARTHUR R DAWES
WILLIAM YOUNG
HUGH McLEAN
MURPHY
L P CARSE
CAINES
CHRISTOPHER NEILSON
FREDERICK HEMMINGSON
CHARLES ANDERSON
ANTOINE
MICHAEL MULLIGAN
JOHN McHUGH

LOST AT SEA OR
INTERNED
ELSEWHERE

JOHN B WALKER
WILLIAM SARP
EDWARD HALE
JOHN CALLAGHAN
JOHN SULLIVAN
WILLIAM COTTER
JEREMIAH O'LEARY
CHARLES JOHNSON
CHARLES RUSSELL

SOLE SURVIVOR
SAMUEL J EVANS

Kate Harding - 1892

Another Wreck on Nauset Beach

A British Bark that ran aground during a storm onto Nauset Beach near Cape Cod Light on November 30, 1892

The Kate Harding on Nauset Beach

S A Rudolph - 1894

Three masted schooner loaded with ice

She was bound for Ocean City, Maryland coming from Boothbay, Maine. Her home port was Philadelphia, PA. and her captain John P Burns of Camden, New Jersey. The ship was caught in a sudden gale on the night of Thursday, April 12th and floundered on the shoals off Nauset Beach.

The fractured hull of the ship washed up north of Nauset Beach. All six crew members perished including Captain Burns and his brother seamen on board the vessel.

Alva - 1892

Vanderbilt Yacht Sinks - Struck by the "Dimock"

narrow escape for the sleeping passengers

Cape Cod 7/24 – Less than a month ago William K. Vanderbilt's magnificent steam yacht *Alva* ran into a pleasure boat in New York Harbor drowning two of its occupants. Yesterday morning, as if in punishment, the *Alva* was run into by the steamer *H. F. Dimock* of the Metropolitan Steamship Lines.

Fortunately not one of the sixty one passengers were killed and only one slightly injured. The Alva had been on a cruise of the Maine coast and had left Bar Harbor at four o'clock Saturday afternoon.

William K. Vanderbilt's steam yacht Alva

 A thick fog had set in by Sunday morning and it had become so dense that the captain decided to drop anchor.

Whistle and horns were blown at frequent intervals and it is said that every precaution was taken to warn other vessels of the *Alva's* whereabouts.

The guests were sleeping in their berths when a heavy crash followed by the sounds of the vessel's plates tearing. Several were tossed from their berths and all made it topside without shoes and wearing only their sleepwear. All were rescued only moments before the *Alva* sank quickly beneath the waves.

Condensed from Boston Evening Transcript article – 7/25/1982

FORTUNA and BARNSTABLE Collide -1896

THE FISHING SCHOONER FORTUNA SUNK BY A COLLISION - NINE SAILORS DROWNED.

Run down by a British steamer. - Fourteen of the crew are saved -- the vessel goes down within three minutes after being struck.

Boston, Jan. 14. -- The fishing schooner *Fortuna*, Capt. GREENLAW, from Boston for St. George's Bank, was in collision last night with British steamer *Barnstable*, off Highland Light. The schooner was cut almost in two, and sank within three minutes. Fourteen of her crew were saved by the steamer, but nine men went down with the vessel. Those drowned belonged in Gloucester, where they leave families.

ARTHUR NOONAN, cook on the fishing vessel, was severely injured by broken timbers, and was sent to the City Hospital. The *Barnatable* is from Port Antonio with fruit for this city. She brought the first intelligence of the disaster when she arrived.

Capt. E. E. PAINE, the commander of the steamer, makes the following report of the collision:

> *"It was about 7:25 o'clock last night, when we were northeast by east, about three miles distant, from Highland Light, Cape Cod. I suddenly discovered a two-masted schooner directly under out port bow. Before anything possible could be done to avert a collision, we crashed into her just abaft of the fore rigging, cutting a great gaping hole in her which extended far below the water line. I immediately ordered the engineer to keep headway in order that the steamer's nose would remain in the aperture made in the schooner long enough to give those on board an opportunity to escape."*

> *"Most of the men on the schooner were in the forecastle, and when the shock of the collision was felt, they hurried on deck, climbed up the rigging of their vessel,*

and reached the deck of the steamer. Nine of them, however, were unable to escape. In about four minutes after the collision occurred the schooner drifted away from the steamer, plunged forward, and sank in about fifty fathoms of water. We remained in the vicinity for some hours, hoping to rescue some of the men, but after a thorough search, no trace of them could be found, so the steamer proceeded."

The *Fortuna* left the wharf at Boston at 1 o'clock yesterday morning, bound for the George's on a fishing trip. She had a crew of twenty-three men, all told, most of them belonging in Gloucester.

Capt. PAINE stated that the weather was clear at the time of the collision, and that the schooner's jib or forestay sail obscured her lights so that it was impossible to see her from the steamer until too late to avoid collision.

The members of the schooner's crew who were saved left their vessel so hurriedly that they were unable to save any of their effects. They were sent to their homes in Gloucester to-day. The steamer sustained no injury, save the scraping of the paint from her bow.

The *Fortuna* was built at Gloucester in 1894. She registered 124 tons gross, and was owned by A. G. HALL of Gloucester. She was fully insured in the Boston Marine Insurance Company for $9,500.

The New York Times New York 1896-01-15

The Monte Tabor – 1896

Italian Bark Wrecked - *The captain& mate lose their wits, commit suicide*. Seven of the Crew Saved by Clinging to the Rigging and Five Are Drowned.

HIGHLAND LIGHT, Mass., Sept. 14.

The Italian bark *Monte Tabor*, loaded with salt, went on Peaked Hill bar at midnight and shortly after began to break up. The crew became panic-stricken. Even the officers lost their wits. The captain, F. Dellacassa, evidently considering himself responsible for the loss of the vessel, shot himself in the head with a revolver and fell dead to the deck, whence his body was soon afterward washed into the sea.

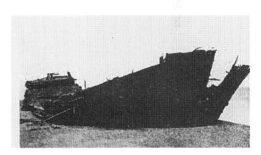

Monte Tabor on the bar

The mate, believing death to be inevitable and afraid of drowning, drew his razor across his throat, producing a ghastly wound and falling dead into the water beside the doomed bark.

The crew, twelve in number, clung to the deckhouse, expecting every minute to be the last. The vessel held together for about an hour and then went to pieces. The twelve men went over the side still clinging to the deckhouse. Five of them, however, were unable to maintain their hold and were soon drowned. The survivors reached the shore in an exhausted condition and were taken to the Peaked Hill life-saving station, where they were cared for. The body of the mate was washed ashore at Race Point at 9 o'clock. An hour and a half later two other bodies were found on the shore. One of these men had followed the example of the mate and had cut his throat before being swept into the sea.

ANNIE E. RUDOLPH - 1897

Sunk off Nauset light - The Schooner *Annie E. Rudolph* Run Down by the Tugboat *Paoli* Yesterday.

VINEYARD HAVEN, Mass., May 9.---The tug *Paoli,* Capt. Harding, brought the news here this afternoon of the collision with and the sinking of the schooner *Annie E. Rudolph* of Camden, N. J., off the Nauset Light, early this morning, and the loss of her skipper, Capt. Gardiner, Mate Snell, and a Norwegian seaman called Bob. The balance of the crew of the Rudolph, consisting of Steward George Brown and a seaman named Johnson, were saved by the crew of the *Paoli.*

The collision between the tug and the schooner took place about three and a half miles southeast of the Three Lights, which surmount the Bluffs of Nauset, and occurred about 3 o'clock this morning. The *Paoli* was on her way from Boston bound for South Amboy with the barges *Braddock, Strafford*, and *Moore* strung out in a long line behind, making a tow of nearly half a mile. The tug left Boston late yesterday afternoon, and the barges being light, made good headway rounding the Cape about midnight, and under a clear sky, proceeded down the coast toward the shoals.

Notwithstanding the clearness of the sky, however, a dull haze hung over the water, limiting the range of vision. The three lights of Nauset were abeam by 3 o'clock, and Capt. Harding was peering out for the two lights at Chatham, when suddenly a schooner loomed up dead ahead. The accounts of the appearance of the schooner are conflicting, and it is said that she carried no lights. Her approach, however, was very sudden, and before the tug could swerve from her course, hampered as she was somewhat by the barges astern, the two vessels came together, the sharp prow of the tug plunging into the schooner's side and tearing a hole into which tons of water rushed.

The schooner careened under the blow of the collision, and almost before the crew of either vessel realized what had occurred, she plunged downward into the depths of the ocean. The crew of the tug was horrified at the sudden disappearance of the schooner. It was but a moment's time for her to back water and, dropping her three barges, the *Paoli* put back to the place where it was thought the schooner had sunk. After a few minutes' search, Steward Brown was picked up, and then Johnson was hauled out of what was almost his watery grave. But this was all that the sea would give up. Somewhere about fifty feet beneath the waves was the skipper, his mate, and the other unfortunate mariner, carried down by the final plunge of their craft.

As soon as the steward recovered sufficiently it was learned that the unfortunate schooner was the *Annie E. Rudolph*, from Camden, N. J., with a load of iron water-pipe for the Boston Water Works. The very weight of this cargo at once accounted for the awful and sudden plunge of the vessel, and probably for the carrying down of the three men, so that the escape of Brown and his companion from being caught was miraculous.

Brown stated to Capt. Harding of the *Paoli* that the *Rudolph* left Camden last week and after an uneventful run from the Delaware Capes passed up into Vineyard. Sound early Saturday morning, and last night she passed through Slue and made the Chatham lights. Just how the accident occurred, however, the steward was unable to state. Whether the lights were lighted or not he could not say. All that he remembers was a deafening crash and then he found himself in the water.

The *Paoli* remained at the scene of the wreck some hours in the hope of picking up the bodies of Capt. Gardiner and his two companions, but nothing was seen of them. All that marked the scene of the awful tragedy were the masts of the *Rudolph*, just sticking up through the waves. The *Paoli* picked up her barges and started on her way, arriving here about noon to-day. She proceeded to her destination to-night. The *Paoli,* which is an iron-built tug, was uninjured in the collision.

The New York Times, New York, NY 10 May 1897

Ardendu and Herman Winter Collide – 1900

STEAMER ARDENDHU SUNK

Rammed by the Herman Winter in Vineyard Sound.

TWO OF VESSEL'S CREW LOST

So Far as Can Be Learned Collision
Was Due to a Misunderstanding of Whistle Signals.

VINEYARD HAVEN, Mass., Jan. 23.—The
Glasgow steamer Ardandhu, on her first
trip on a new line from New London to
Halifax and thence to Havana, was sunk by
the Metropolitan liner Herman Winter, Boston for New York, off Robinson's Hole,
Vineyard Sound, early this morning, and
two men of a crew of thirty-one were lost.
The Herman Winter made this port this
morning with her bow badly stove in and
carrying the twenty-nine survivors of the
lost steamship.

The Glasgow vessel was struck about
amidships on her starboard side by the Herman Winter's bow. and was cut half way
through. She would have sunk immediately,
but her watertight compartments kept her
afloat for a time. The crew made a rush,
and it was thought that all had succeeded in

January 23, 1900

The misunderstanding of whistle signals is said to have led to the collision of the steamer Arendhu and the freighter *Herman Winter* in Vineyard Sound, just off southwest end of Naushon Island.

Forty four years later the *Herman Winter* ran aground not far from the site of the collision with the *Ardendhu* at Devils Bridge reef, off Gay Head, Martha's Vineyard. The wreck is mostly broken up but easily accessible by divers at a depth of forty feet.

Herman Winter

John S. Parker -1901

Ran aground on Nauset Beach

This three masted schooner was carrying lumber from Nova Scotia bound for New York when she ran aground in a November 7, 1901 gale. The crew was rescued by lifesavers from the U.S. Lifesaving Station at Pochet Island, using the breeches buoy rescue equipment. That station no longer exists.

JOHN S. PARKER, WHICH BECAME A TOTAL LOSS ON NAUSET BARS.

In 2001 a March northeaster exposed remains of the *John S. Parker* on Nauset barrier beach for a short period and then the "bones" of the wooden vessel were quickly sanded over again.

Chatham Life Savers Perish – 1902

You have to go out but - You don't have to return

It was a cold day in March 1902 when a tragedy that would shake all of New England began to unfold. Two coal barges, the *Fitzpatrick* and the *Wadena*, had been stranded on Shovelful Shoals off Monomoy Point for several days.

Many of the crews had been taken off by the Monomoy life-saving team. Wreckers went aboard as the weather allowed to begin salvaging the vessels and their cargos.

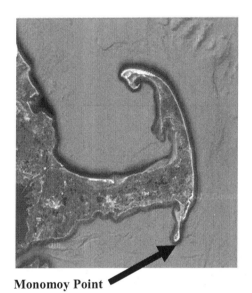

Monomoy Point

On the evening of March 16 the weather began to deteriorate and all but a few men were taken off the barges.

By morning the surf was running very high and the bargemen raised the distress signal. A surfboat was launched into the extremely rough sea. The surfboat reached the relative calm the lee side of the barge provided and began to load the frightened bargemen aboard.

As they pulled away from the barge a huge wave caught up the surfboat capsizing her. The bargemen were washed away to drown. The boat was capsized and righted several times each time sending lifesavers to a watery grave until the five bargemen and eight surfmen had perished.

Sole Survivor's Account of the Chatham Tragedy

Schooner Barges *Wadena* and *Fitzpatrick* aground on Shovelful Shoals, off Monomoy Island

Seth Ellis, Keeper of the Monomy Island Lifesaving Station's account of the tragic events mid March, 1902 as recorded in his log.

"On Tuesday, March 11, 1902, about one o'clock A.M. the schooner barge Wadena stranded during a northeast gale and heavy seas on the Shovelful Shoal, off the southern end of Monomoy Island. The crew was rescued by our station crew. The barge remained on the shoal without signs of going to pieces, and wreckers were engaged in lightening her cargo of coal. On the night of March 16 the weather became threatening, and all except five of the persons engaged in lightening the cargo were taken ashore from the barge by the tug Peter Smith, which was in the employ of the owners of the barge.

"Shortly before eight o'clock on the morning of March 17 on of the patrolmen from our station reported that the Wadena appeared to be in no immediate danger, but later Captain Eldredge received a message from Hyannis, inquiring whether everything was all right with the men on the barge over night.

"Upon receipt of this inquiry Captain Eldredge, putting on his hip boots and oils clothes, set out for the end of the Point, where he could personally ascertain the conditions.

"Arriving there he found that the barge was flying a signal of distress. He at once telephoned me, as I was the No. 1 man at the station, directing me to launch the surf boat from the inside of the beach, and with the crew pull down to the Point. About two and one-0half miles south of the station we took Captain Eldredge aboard and I gave him the steering oar.

"The wind was fresh from the southeast and there was a heavy sea running, but all the crew were of the opinion that the condition of the Wadena was not perilous, as she seemed to be sound and lying easy.

"Captain Eldredge decided to pull around the Point to the barge. At certain places on the shoals the sea was especially rough, and some water was shipped on the way out to the distressed craft, but without any trouble we succeeded in bringing our surfboat under the lee of the barge just abaft the fore rigging, the only place where it was practical to go alongside.

"As soon as we got alongside the barge a line was thrown aboard and made fast by the persons on board. The persons on board were all excited and wanted us to take them ashore as soon as we could. Captain Eldredge, without a moment's delay, when he found out the number of persons on board the barge and their desire to be taken ashore, directed them to get into the surfboat

"The seas were breaking heavily around the stern of the barge, and there was little room for operations in the smooth water, and the rail of the barge was twelve or thirteen feet above the surf-boat. Four of the five men lowered themselves over the side of the barge, one at a time, into the surf-boat, without mishap, by means of a rope, but the captain of the barge, who was a big, heavy man, let go his hold when part way down and dropped into the boat with such force as to break the after thwart. All five being safely in the boat, two were placed forward, two aft, and one amidships, and told to sit quietly and keep close down in the bottom of the boat.

"In order to get away from the barge quickly the painter was cut, by orders of the Captain Eldredge, and the surf-boat was at once shoved off. In order to clear the line of breakers that extended from the stern of the barge so we could lay a good course for the shore.. a part of the surfmen were backing hard on the port oars, while the others gave way with full power on the starboard side. Before we could bet the boat turned around a big wave struck us with fearful force, and quite a lot of water poured into the surf-boat.

"Captain Eldredge stood in the stern of the boat with the steering oar in his hand giving orders, and the surfmen stuck to their posts.

"As soon as the water came into the boat, the rescued men jumped up, and becoming panic stricken, threw their arms about the necks of the surfmen so that none of us could use our oars. The seas, one after another, struck us, and the boat, filling with water, turned bottom up, throwing us all into the raging sea. The seas kept striking us after the boat was upset, and we were soon in among the heaviest breakers. Twice we righted the boat, but the seas which struck her before we could get in, capsized her each time.

Barges Wadena and Fitzpatrick Stranded on Shoals at Monomy

"After righting the boat twice, our strength was fast leaving us, and we all knew that we could not last long without assistance. The five men that we had taken off the barge were the first to be swept off the overturned boat and to perish before our eyes. They did not regain hold of the boat after she turned the first time, and were quickly swept to their death.

All of us clung to the boat, giving each other all the encouragement that we could. Surfman Chase was the first one of our crew to perish, then Nickerson and Small were

89

swept to their death. Captain Eldredge, Surfman Kendrick, Foye and Rogers and myself still managed to hold to the boat. Every sea which struck the boat swept completely over us, almost smothering us. Kendrick was the next one of our crew to perish and poor Foye soon followed him. Captain Eldredge and Surfman Rogers and myself were the only ones left, and we expected that we, too, would soon follow the fate of our comrades.

"Rogers was clinging to the boat about midships, while Captain Eldredge and myself were holding on near the stern. Captain Eldredge called to me to help him get a better hold, and I managed to pull him on to the bottom of the boat, when a sea struck us and washed us both off. I managed to regain a hold on the bottom of the boat, and looking around for Captain Eldredge, I saw that he was holding on to the spar and sail which had drifted from underneath the boat, but was still fast to it. The seas were washing me off the boat continually at this time, and when I last saw our brave Captain, he was drifting away from the boat, holding on to the spar and sail.

"My strength was fast going, and when poor Rogers begged me to help him climb further up the boat, the only thing I could do was to tell him that we were drifting towards the beach, and that help would soon be at hand and to hold on.

"Rogers had lost his strength, however, and failing to get a more secure place on the bottom of the boat, feebly moaning, "I have got to go," he fell off the boat and sank beneath the waters.

"I was now alone on the bottom of the boat, and seeing that the center board had slipped partway out, I managed to get hold of it, and holding it with one hand succeeded in getting my oil clothes, undercoat, vest and boots off.

"By that time the overturned boat had drifted down over the shoals in the direction of the barge Fitzpatrick, which was also stranded on the shoals, and when I sighted the craft I waved my hand as a signal for help. I soon saw those on the barge fling a dory over the side into the water, but could see nothing

more of the dory after that on account of the mist and high sea until it hove in sight with a man in it rowing towards me.

"The man in the dory was brave Capt. Elmer F. Mayo. He ran the dory alongside me, and with his help I got into the boat. I was so used up that I was speechless, and all that I could do was knell in the bottom of the boat and hold on to the thwarts. To land in the dory through the surf was a perilous undertaking, but Mayo, who is a skilled boatman, carefully picked his way over the rips and headed his little boat for shore.

"Surfman Bloomer of our station, who had been left ashore, had walked down to the Point to assist Captain Eldredge and crew in landing, and when he saw Mayo fighting his way through the breakers, he ran down into the surf, seized the little boat, and helped Mayo to land safely.

Bloomer was told of the terrible tragedy by Captain Mayo, as I was unable to speak at the time. As I have often said, "If the persons we took off the barge had kept quiet as we told them to, all hands would have been landed in safety."

Seth L. Ellis
Keeper, Monomoy L. S. Station

Oben Shiverick, John E. Ellis, Joseph Bloomer, Captain Kelly, Richard Ryder, Charles Hamilton, Steven Eldredge, Edwin Clark

Elsie M Smith - 1902

Fishing Boat Tragedy

February 14th - Sch. *Elsie M. Smith* was wrecked on Chatham bar, Cape Cod, near Monomoy Point Lighthouse in a blinding snowstorm, while engaged in the haddock fishery.

Dean Doucette, 23, single, and Sylvania Doucette, 27, single, natives of Tusket, N. S., attempted to row ashore and were drowned by the capsizing of their dory. The other sixteen members of the crew stayed with the vessel and were saved.

James P. Smith, a native of Copenhagen, was the keeper of Monomoy Lighthouse along with his three daughters who assisted him in his duties. The oldest daughter, Annie, acted as housekeeper and tended the light when her father was away.

Newspaper report at the time reported:

> *Keeper James Smith, Monomoy Point Lighthouse keeper and his daughters recovered the body of a Nova Scotia fisherman from the wrecked vessel Elsie M. Smith. The man's clothes had filled with sand, and Emma Smith said that he must have weighed 300 pounds. It took Keeper Smith and daughters Annie and Emma to pull the body from the surf.*

**The French named Monomoy Island
"Cape Malabar" or the "Cape of Evil Bars"**

Wentworth - Oct 1904

12 LOST WITH SHIP SHATTERED ON ROCKS.

Gale drove three-master *Wentworth* on Massachusetts coast and bodies of dead washed ashore at feet of life-savers unable to aid.

Chatham, Mass., Oct. 14. -- After battling all night on the bar outside Chatham, the three-masted schooner *Wentworth*, from Hillsboro, N.B., for New York, went to pieces today and eight men, one woman and three children are known to have perished in the wreck.

The captain's wife and three children were the other victims. This ship, laden with plaster, came in last night in the teeth of a gale. For three days the wind from the northeast has blown hard and waves have smashed high up on the bar. It was almost impossible for any ship to live in such a storm close to the shore, and when the vessel was seen at Nantucket Light, ten miles to the north, last evening, running before the gale, those who saw her marveled. Even then she seemed running straight to destruction.

In her cabins the lights were burning brightly and then it was seen that her lights were burning fore and aft. Down the coast came the vessel. That she was heavy was plain. The waves washed over her and many times those on shore saw her dig her nose deep into the ocean, only to rise again and right herself. The wind was blowing with great violence and the waves, close to shore where she was running, were breaking over her, smashing her cabins and threatening to carry away her decks

Then the schooner came into the bar. She struck with a force and a grating that could be heard above the noise of the wind and the waves.

Instantly the seas rolled over her and pitched her further up on the rocks. Then there came signals of distress from the vessel.
The men on board were evidently in desperate straits, for they signaled often. Men on sea-going schooners do not signal

repeatedly for distress when these signals are answered from shore unless they are in dire need of help.

Then there gathered on the shore Capt. Doane with the rest of the life-saving crew from Old Harbor. Attempts were made to launch a lifeboat. The waves smashed the boat as though it were made of tissue paper. A gun was placed on shore and the breeches buoy was shot out to the schooner in distress.

Then there came a wave over the vessel. Those on shore could see the water as it rolled far above her decks. The lights in the cabin went out. The lights fore and aft were washed away, and all on board the vessel was quiet.

Until dawn the life-savers worked, but their efforts were futile. There was not an answer to their cries, not an effort made to fasten the line as it was shot across the ship.

As the ship gave way, with a sound like the bursting of cannon the body of a woman was caught in the whirl of the tide and thrown up on the shore where the life-savers stood. Then came the body of a man.

By this time the ship was in pieces. She was rent in twain and broken to splinters. The *Wentworth* was in command of Capt. PREDDLE and carried a crew of seven men. Capt. PREDDLE'S wife was also aboard, and it is supposed it was her body that was washed ashore

The captain also had his three small children aboard when he left on his voyage, and these are counted lost. The woman whose body was washed ashore was about thirty-two years old. She was fully dressed and had on an outside cloak. On one finger was a heavy plain gold ring. Her face was considerably disfigured, probably from contact with the wreckage. The man was about thirty-five years old, and was fully clad except that he wore no coat.

William H. Edgett, of Moncton, N.B., was the owner of the schooner. The *Wentworth*, with her cargo of plaster, was valued at $8,000. Both vessel and cargo were insured.

The Evening World New York 1904-10-14

The Aransas - 1905

Collides with schooner barge

Passenger ship collided with the schooner barge *Glendower* at
Pollock Rip, off Chatham in a fog, on May 7, 1905. One
passenger was lost and the wreck blown up to reduce
navigation hazard. Large sections of wreck remain partially
buried in sand.

The Aransas

JOY LINE STEAMER SUNK IN COLLISION

Aransas Hits Barge Off Pollock's Rip—Woman Passenger Lost.

BOATS MANNED PROMPTLY

Steamer Was Bound from Boston to New York—Crash Occurred in a Fog.

Dolphin Explosion - Jul 1907

LAUNCH BLOWS UP - FOUR MEN KILLED IN SAD ACCIDENT OFF MARION, MASS, TWO OTHERS ARE SAVED

Picked Up After Being in Water Twelve Hours
"Victims Were Prominent Citizens"

Marion, Mass. " Four prominent summer residents of this town and Falmouth met death through an explosion on board a 45-foot launch off here Saturday night. Two survivors were picked up Sunday after having been in the water for 12 hours.

The dead: ROLAND WORTHINGTON, Boston; JOHN T. TRULL, Woburn; JOSEPH S. BEAL, Milton, and GEORGE SAVORY, Marblehead, captain of the launch.

The saved: A. P. Tarbell, Marblehead and Edward Pecker, Boston.

Pecker, who was clinging to an oar, and Tarbell, who was supported by a life preserver, were able to swim, and they remained together until picked up by a lobster fisherman going out in the early morning to haul his pots.

Mr. Tarbell, who owned the *Dolphin,* as the launch was called, said the boat started out from Marion on a short pleasure cruise and was well out in the middle of Buzzards Bay when the explosion occurred. Savory, the engineer, was suddenly blown into the air and was probably dead when he struck the water.

The boat caught fire immediately and Tarbell called to his comrades to leap overboard. He strapped a life preserver about himself before he leaped, and Mr. Pecker, who is connected with the Boston banking firm of Rollins & Sons, seized an oar and followed. So far as they knew, none of the others in the party jumped. Either they could not swim and preferred to cling to the disabled launch until help came, or else they were stunned by the explosion.

The Stevens Point Journal, Stevens Point, WI 18 Jul 1908

S. S. Onondaga - 1907

Hard upon Chatham Beach

Chatham, MA - January 13, 1907 The American Steamer *Onondaga*, bound from Boston to Jacksonville, Florida ran aground on Nauset Beach in dense fog.

Life-Savers from the Old Harbor Station responded and hauled out the breeches buoy, but as the seas had calmed none of the crew were landed at that time. The vessel remained for three months when in March the steamer was refloated, with the aid of tugboats.

In order to pull the steamer from the beach, she had to be lightened and unloaded by hand.

Cargo being off loaded by hand

Horatio Hall - 1909

The "Dimock" Strikes Again

On March 10, 1909, the *H.F. Dimock*, bound from New York to Boston, and the coastwise steamer *Horatio Hall* of the Maine Steamship Company collided in the eastern Vineyard Sound shortly after 8 a.m. while sailing at half speed in a heavy fog.

Horatio Hall

The accident occurred in Pollock Rip Slue, not far from where the *H.F. Dimock* had collided with the *Alva* in 1892. Captain John A. Thompson of the *H.F. Dimock* brough his vessel alongside the *Horatio Hall* so that the latter's five passengers could be transferred.

Most of her crew left in lifeboats and were picked up by the *H.F. Dimock*, but Captain W. Frank Jewell, the pilot, first mate, and two seamen remained in the pilot house, which remained a few feet above water. (They were picked up later.) The *H.F. Dimock* left the scene at 11:15 a.m. and sailed slowly toward Orleans Life-Saving Station, where she was beached.

The passengers and crew were removed by the lifesavers under Captain James H. Charles. Moderately damaged, the *H.F. Dimock* was later hauled off the beach and towed to shipyard for repairs.

PAUL PALMER - 1913

Caught Fire and Sank on Stellwagen Bank

Built in Waldoboro, Maine, the five-masted, 276-foot schooner *Paul Palmer* was part of William F. Palmer's "Great White Fleet," which at its peak consisted of 15 schooners that carried bulk cargos throughout the East Coast, Gulf of Mexico, and Caribbean. During its 12-year career, the schooner *Paul Palmer* transported 280,000 tons of coal, as well as phosphate, railroad ties, ice, and sugar.

The launching of the Paul Palmer in Waldoboro, ME - 1902

"The schooner's involvement in the coal trade connected it to Americans throughout the East Coast," said Stellwagen Bank sanctuary Superintendent Craig MacDonald. "Coal carried in schooners like the *Paul Palmer* powered the industrialization of the northeastern states, one of the greatest economic and social forces in American history."

After unloading coal in Bangor, *Paul Palmer* departed Rockport, Maine, for Virginia on Friday, June 13, 1913. Sailing south, the schooner caught fire off Cape Cod. Several vessels responded to the stricken schooner, but were unable to extinguish the fire. The schooner's crew abandoned ship and was picked up by a waiting fishing boat. The *Paul Palmer* burned to its waterline and then sank. The *Paul Palmer* was the only five-masted East Coast schooner to be lost to fire.

The passengers of the *Palmer* took to lifeboats and were picked up by the schooner *Rose Dorothea*, bringing the victims into Provincetown. The *Palmer* finally succumbed to the flames in the evening hours and sank, with her masts and rigging partially exposed breaching the surface.

The *Paul Palmer* was no stranger to fire. In 1907, the schooner sustained light damage when it was nearly caught in a conflagration that consumed Baltimore's coal docks. The following year, a fire swept across East Boston's docks, catching the schooner's top rigging afire. Tugs pulled *Paul Palmer* away from its dock and put out the fire before flames engulfed the schooner. The fire destroyed a quarter-mile stretch of the waterfront and caused $1.6 million in property damage.

The Palmer's winch

The cause of the sinking was not immediately known and the Coast Guard cutter *Androscoggin* was dispatched from Portland, ME to destroy the remnants of the hulk so as to avoid a hazard to navigation.

Today, the *Paul Palmer* sits in approximately 85 feet of water on the southern portion of Stellwagen Bank NMS. As the hull nearly burned completely prior to sinking, the remaining amount of wreckage is small. The wreck site mainly consists of a "footprint" of a large schooner with the largest beams of the keel running down the centerline of the wreck. The chain pile and winch are evident in the bow, and a small section of hull comes up along the port side in several places.

Leonora Silveria - 1921

One Died and 17 Were Saved.

The schooner Leonora Silveira ran aground at Peaked Hill Bars, Cape Cod. November 6, 1921.

The *Leonora Silveira*, a Boston based schooner, wrecked on Peaked Hill Bars, Mass and was battered by the waves. Seaman Edward Mose perished but the Coast Guards took off the other seventeen members of the crew with the breeches buoy.

Aground on Nauset Beach

The Schooner Montclair - 1927

The skeleton of the schooner the *Montclair*, which was stranded and wrecked on Nauset Beach in March 1927, re-emerged from the sand, according a report in the Cape Cod Times. Shipwreck guru William Quinn of Orleans, who saw the wreckage the last time it was exposed by the elements in 1957, made that identification after looking over the wreckage.

The timbers were exposed after a storm but Mother Nature, with her tides and winds, had buried her in the sand again within a few days.

Ship wreckage and other artifacts often turn up on the beaches of the Cape, but that this was the first time the

The Montclair on Nauset Beach in 1927

Montclair had been seen since the vessel first broke apart in 1927.

For more history on the *Montclair*, one need only turn to Chapter 6 of Henry Beston's book, *The Outermost House*. In the chapter, *Lanterns on the Beach*, Beston chronicles the event:

"There has just been a great wreck, the fifth this winter and the worst. On Monday morning last, shortly after five o'clock, the big three-masted schooner Montclair stranded at Orleans and went to pieces in an hour, drowning five of her crew."

The remains of the *Montclair* exposed on Nauset Beach in 2010

The *Montclair*, bound for New York from Halifax, had a crew of seven. The two survivors were a sailor and a 17-year-old boy. Beston later wrote that the boy "is dead of the shock and exposure."

The sailor decides he's going on with life at sea. "It's all he knows," a coast guardsman told Beston. The wreck was visible from the deck of Beston's "Fo'castle," his 20×16 house on Coast Guard Beach in Eastham. The horror of the wreck endured as well, as Beston wrote:

"A week after the wreck, a man walking the Orleans shore came to a lonely place, and there he saw ahead of him a hand thrust up out of the great sands. Beneath he found the buried body of one of the Montclair's crew."

Schooner, AVALON - 1927

FISHING BOAT SUNK OFF CAPE COD. - 11 LIVES LOST IN COLLISION EARLY TODAY.

BIG STEAMER "*PRESIDENTE WILSON*" COLLIDED WITH THE GLOCESTER SCHOONER "AVALON" IN DENSE FOG.

The "Avalon" Was On Way To Fishing Grounds. While The Steamer Had Left New York For Boston Friday Night -- Schooner Sunk Almost Immediately.

Boston, Oct. 29 -- (UP) -- Nosing slowly through a dense fog, the steamer *Presidente Wilson*, with 552 passengers aboard, rammed and sank the Gloucester fishing schooner "*Avalon*" of Cape Cod early today, with a possible loss of 11 lives.

Only three members of the two-master's crew were safe aboard the big steamship five hours after the crash, which occurred about five miles off Highland Light. Two bodies had been recovered.

Radio dispatches to the United Press from the master of the *Presidente Wilson* reported nine men still missing. The steamer reported it was standing by in the hope of picking up other members of the "*Avalon's*" crew, but a fog blanket was handicapping the *Presidente Wilson*.

The "*Avalon*" a two master which had put out from Boston yesterday was enroute to the fishing grounds when the big steamer sent it to the bottom. Details of the collision were not available early this morning, but radio reports from the scene of the crash indicated that the schooner had sunk almost immediately.

The following radio message was received today from the master of the steamer *Presidente Wilson* which this morning collided with and sank a fishing schooner off Cape Cod, Mass.: "Picked up two bodies" "Nine men missing." "Ship still standing by." "Master"

Dunkirk Evening Observer New York 1927-10-29

SS Robert E. Lee disaster - 1928

Three of Station No. 31's Guardsmen, Boatswain's Mate William Cashman and Surfmen Edward Stark and Frank Griswold, drowned after assisting the stricken passenger liner *SS Robert E. Lee.* The Boston-to-New York-bound steamer, with 273 passengers and crew, grounded on the treacherous Mary Ann Rocks just southeast of Manomet Point during a gale at about 8 p.m. on Saturday, March 9, 1928.

Boston Globe March 11, 1928

Seven oarsman and Cashman tried again and again to reach the stricken ship via their oar-powered surf boat, but were held back by raging seas. (They were unaware that passengers and crew did not appear to be in imminent danger because the captain had securely scuttled the ship on the rocks). The Guardsmen ultimately reached the liner on March 10 and assisted in rescue efforts. The Guardsmen were on a return trip to the station when their surf boat overturned in "an unusually ponderous sea." Three drowned.

> *"It was only one of the thousands of seas that the lifeboat had ridden buoyantly during the morning. But it caught her in a shoal place and it was an unusually ponderous sea. Its foot 'tripped' on the bottom and it towered high in the air, tilting the boat's bow down and flinging Cashman almost above the heads of his seven oarsmen.*
>
> *Then the wave broke at the crest, and the boat was whirled over, the men dropping out, clutching at one another and at the great oars that were tumbling down with them. Hundreds of people were watching the boat, and a great cry went up from the crowd. People began to run down to the bowlder - strewn beach, helplessly enough, in their distress."*

A number of young men watching from the shore secured small rowboats and rushed out to the stricken surf boat. Those rescuers were later awarded Carnegie Medals for bravery.

Stark died en route to a Boston hospital; Cashman died on the beach after lengthy resuscitation by a doctor, and Griswold's body eventually washed ashore about two miles away. The five others were treated at hospitals in Plymouth and Chelsea.

Memorial marker

A memorial plaque and stone monument for the fallen 3 heroes was installed at the tip of Manomet Point in May, 1928 by the citizens of Plymouth. It reads:

In memory of Boatswain's Mate William H. Cashman, Surfman Frank W. Griswold, Surfman Edward P. Stark, who of Station No. 31 United States Coast Guard lost their lives in the performance of their duty, March 10, 1928, when the Steamship Robert E. Lee stranded on the Mary Ann Rocks Southeast of this station.

Greater love hath no man than this that a man lay down his life for his friends.

**Memorial Stone at the tip of
Monument Point**

SS Stephen R. Jones – 1942

Sunk inside the Cape Cod Canal – Closing it for nearly a Month

At 3AM on June 28, 1942 and the *S.S. Stephen R. Jones* struck the north bank of the Cape Cod Canal 2,000 feet east of the Bourne Bridge and sank by the bow. This caused the closure of the Canal to all military and commercial traffic. Some believe the Germans had sabotaged this vessel in order to close the Canal, thereby diverting shipping outside via the lightship channel.

S.S. STEPHEN R. JONES sunk in the Cape Cod Canal

Attempts to raise the vessel with cranes and barge failed and for 28 days, all shipping had to go through the Lightship channel and Pollock Rip or the Main Channel via Great Round Shoal out to the North Atlantic or were forced outside coming around the Cape from Boston to New York. Either way, they steamed right into the breech of the Wolf Pack waiting with their torpedoes off the backside of Cape Cod.

Finally a solution was found. They would dynamite a large hole underneath the stricken vessel into which the ship would be allowed to settle. It remains on the bottom of the Canal to this day. You can locate just where it lies by the magnetic anomaly caused by the ship's rusting iron hull lying on the bottom.

SS James Longstreet - 1944

Target Ship in Cape Cod Bay

The *SS James Longstreet was* named after the Confederate general of the same name and was a familiar sight in Cape Cod Bay for more than fifty years.

SS Longstreet as a Target Ship

This World War II Liberty Ship was severely damaged off Long Island on October 26, 1943 when gale force winds drove her onto the sand flats of Sandy Neck, New Jersey.

She ran aground at a flood tide so when the tide went out the steamer was high and dry. The damage was very extensive and so it wasn't until the end of November that she was refloated and towed to New York.

It was there that the Navy declared her a "Constructive Total Loss." Instead of being scrapped, the US Navy used her as a test ship until it was decided she would be used as a target ship.

She was towed to Cape Cod and grounded three and a half miles off Rock Harbor in Orleans and used as a target ship for early air to surface guided missiles. Later she was used for live ammunition target practice by naval jets from nearby South Weymouth Naval Air Station and the Air Force from Cape Cod's Otis Air Force Base until 1971.

The remains of the *James Longstreet* lie in approximately 20 to 25 feet of water. The site is off limits to divers due to unexploded ordnance.

First known photograph of the SS James Longstreet. Snapped Oct 7, 1943 at Southampton, England - the day she started on the last leg of her third and final voyage.
National Maritime Museum, London, England

The "April Fool's" blizzard of 1997 covered the last traces of the old target ship. For awhile she was still visible from the air but no longer.

SS Longstreet before disappearing into the sandy shoal off Eastham

Two Tankers Break in Half Within 40 Miles of Each Other - 1952

On February 18, 1952 two 520' T-2 tankers broke in half within 40 miles of each other. The tankers were east of Cape Cod in a raging storm with 70-knot winds and 60-foot seas. The *Pendleton* out of Baton Rouge, Louisiana, bound for Boston, Massachusetts, carrying kerosene and heating oil broke apart at dawn.

The *Fort Mercer*, also carrying kerosene, and bound for Portland, Maine, began to break apart later that morning about 8:00AM. The *Fort Mercer* sent an "SOS," but the initial break caused *Pendelton* to lose all radio capability, and for eight terrible hours, before she was discovered, she waited in silence for help she had no reason to believe would ever come.

FORT MERCER, Feb 18 at 8:00a.m. 1952

Coast Guard cutters *Eastwind*, *Unimak*, *Yakutat*, *Achushnet*, *McCulloch*, two 36' motor lifeboats, numerous aircraft and additional Coast Guard craft and personnel were on their way.

From the December 27, 1952 issue of Collier's - " *The Acushnet had been ordered to sea at noon the day before. At the time she had been laid up, with her engines partially dismantled and her crew scattered throughout the snowbound city of Portland. Yet three hours later she was on her way, with every man of the crew*

Acushnet rescues crew from the Fort Mercer

110

aboard....Joseph (Lieutenant Commander John M. Joseph) let the Acushnet drift towards the Fort Mercer.

Then turning his bow out and easing his stern quarter toward the larger vessel, he closed the gap. The trick was to get near enough for a man to jump across and still keep the two wildly rolling, pitching ships from grinding together. The Acushnet got five men on her first pass; then the sea knocked her out of position.

Joseph signaled full speed ahead and circled around again. '....This time I really had it.' he remembers with satisfaction. 'My ship came right in on Fort Mercer's stern section and I held her there while we took off thirteen more. We could have taken everyone aboard on that pass but no one else wanted to leave. "

"After the breakup, the engines on the stern section (Fort Mercer) had continued to run: by the time they were ordered stopped by Chief Engineer Jesse Bushnell of

Coast Guard Cutter YAKUTAT puts over a motor self-bailing surfboat to remove two ill survivors from the bow of the S.S. FORT MERCER."

Pasadena, Texas, senior officer on the stern, the two sections had become widely separated. But suddenly the bow driven by the screaming wind bore down on the stern and a collision seemed imminent. In a maneuver undoubtedly unique in marine history, Bushnell ordered full speed astern and narrowly escaped being sunk by the front of his own ship!"

At first the Coast Guard knew of only one shipwreck. Even after the second split tanker was discovered from the air, almost by accident (its radio had been ruined before a distress message could be sent), officials directing the operation found it hard to believe that they actually had a double disaster to deal with."

From VADM Benedict L. Stabiles's notes on the reverse side of a photograph of the Fort Mercer's bow- "Bow of Fort Mercer after capsizing. 20 minutes after last man was removed it capsized. Was later sunk by gunfire and depth charges. As far as I know the Fort Mercer is the only vessel in history whose bow was sunk by the combined effort of 40mm projectiles striking the bottom or keel side of the vessel and depth charges damaging the top or deck side. Further I presume it is the first modern vessel that has been sunk by broadside fire. The CGC Unimak *steamed alongside with ENS B.L. Stabile in charge of the starboard battery applying Kentucky windage & radar range and with one well placed salvo of MK-9 depth charges sank the bow section."*

The *Boston Globe* put out an EXTRA edition with vivid accounts of the daring rescues. The *Boston Herald* too had multiple pages devoted to the rescues and aerial photographs of the ships involved.

According to these newspaper accounts- While less than 6 miles off of Chatham, *McCulloch* was first on the scene of the foundering bow of *Pendleton.* She could not get close enough to attempt a rescue because of the shoals. A 36 ft motor lifeboat (MLB) arrived and was putting out rafts, and they watched as the lone survivor on the bow cast himself into the sea too soon and was lost.

Two survivors being pulled from rubber raft

The *Yakutat* too was involved in the rescue. She completed the rescue of the remaining four men from the bow of *Fort Mercer* less than twenty minutes before it capsized. The following information was on the reverse side of an official Coast Guard photograph-

"The Yakutat spent the night of the 18ᵗʰ trying to shoot lines to the bow section of Fort Mercer. The 50 knot winds and 35 foot swells foiled all attempts at rescue operations. At daylight next morning, the motor surfboat was lowered, and it fought its way to Fort Mercer's Bow. The men would have to jump overboard and be taken aboard the monomoy. The crew of Mercer wanted the ailing master to jump overboard first because of his weakened condition. He was reluctant to leave his ship but the crew said he must jump or they would throw him overboard. He jumped and he was picked up. As the surfboat snatched a second man from the sea it was dashed into the side of the Fort Mercer's bow. Damaged and leaking, it was forced to return to the Yakutat. That it was able to return, was considered a miracle in itself. The remaining two men were rescued by means of rubber rafts, with all too few minutes to spare."

The saga of the *Fort Mercer* did not end there in that terrible storm off Cape Cod. The stern portion of the *Fort Mercer* lived to sail again. According to the *Houston Chronicle* June 7, 1964-"The *Fort Mercer's* stern was used to build a new tanker, the *San Jacinto*. The *San Jacinto* broke in half off the Virginia coast on March 26, 1964.

The 'Fort Mercer Stern' divested itself of yet another bow, and remained afloat! Will the Coast Guard meet her again?"

PENDLETON Feb. 18 at 5:50 a.m. - 1952

The 503-foot, 10,448 gross ton tank vessel *Pendleton* was built by the Kaiser Company in 1944 and departed Baton Rouge, LA on February 12, 1952 with cargo of 122,000 barrels of kerosene and heating oil. The ship carried a crew of 41, including the master, Captain John Fitzgerald.

Late on the evening of 17 February, *Pendleton* arrived off Boston. The weather was foul with extremely limited visibility. The captain opted to stand off and headed his vessel east-northeast at slow speed into Massachusetts Bay. The wind and sea conditions worsened throughout the night, building into a full-scale 'Nor'easter' gale with snow and high seas.

By 4:00 a.m. on February 18, *Pendleton* began shipping seas over her stern, but the vessel appeared to be riding well. Sometime after 4 a.m., the vessel rounded the tip of Cape Cod off Provincetown, MA and assumed a more southerly course.

At about 5:50 a.m. on 18 February, after a series of explosive cracking noises, the *Pendleton* took a heavy lurch and broke in two. At the time of the break, the vessel's circuit breakers tripped, leaving the bow section without power. The stern section continued to operate normally, including all machinery and lighting.

The Pendleton's bow section

Gone with the darkened bow section were the Captain and seven other crewmen, all of whom were destined to perish. In the stern, was the Chief Engineer, Raymond Sybert, and 32 crewmen.

Alone, adrift, in mountainous seas, the stern section and its human cargo drifted south with a slight port list about six miles off Cape Cod. The bow section also drifted south, but at a further distance offshore. No S.O.S. had been issued.

The Rescue

At noon, the station Officer in Charge, Bos'n Cluff, ordered Chief Bos'n Mate Donald Bangs to select his crew and man the *CG-36383* motor life boat (MLB) at Stage Harbor and proceed to assist the *Fort Mercer*. At the time, Bos'n Mate 1st Class (BM1) Webber who had remained behind, thought:

"My God, do they really think a lifeboat and its crew could actually make it that far out to sea in this storm and find the broken ship amid the blinding snow and raging seas with only a compass to guide them? If the crew of the lifeboat didn't freeze to death first, how would they be able to get the men off the storm-tossed sections of the broken tanker?" He would soon find out.

On the stern section of the *Pendleton*, Engineer Sybert's crew sighted the beach at about two p.m. At 2:55 p.m., the Chatham Lifeboat Station's (CLS)' radar picked up two blips about five and a half miles distant. At 3:00 p.m., Bos'n Cluff visually sighted the bow section of the *Pendleton*. Cluff's report to the Boston regional Coast Guard headquarters caused Coast

Motorized lifeboat (MLB) leaves to assist the Pendleton

Guard PBY aircraft No. 1242 to be diverted from ongoing rescue operations further offshore involving the *Fort Mercer*. Shortly after 4 p.m., the PBY made the first positive identification of both sections of the *Pendleton*. The Coast Guard now knew for the first time it had <u>two</u> stricken T2 tankers and four different possible rescue situations.

The *Pendleton*'s stern section and its crew of 33 drifted close to shore. Close enough that local residents could occasionally hear the ship's whistle and see the vessel as it galloped along up and down huge waves, frothing each time it rose or settled back into the sea.

Bos'n Cluff then ordered, "Webber, pick yourself a crew. Y'all got to take the 36500 out over the bar and assist that thar ship, ya-heah?" With great trepidation having seen the conditions offshore and knowing his likely fate, but understanding his duty, he replied, "Yes sir, Mr. Cluff, I'll get ready." It was time to choose his crew. Only three men were available.

At 5:55 p.m., Webber and his last-minute-crew left the pier in their wooden 36-foot-long motorized lifeboat driven along by its single 90 horsepower gas engine. As coxswain, Webber

Stern of the Pendleton in calm waters

turned his lifeboat into the channel, he could see the station's lights and hoped for a hasty recall. Hearing nothing, he radioed the station and received the curt response "Proceed as directed." Back on the *Pendleton's* stern, Engineer Sybert saw the stern section headed for grounding on Chatham's bar and certain disaster. Sybert used the tanker's engines to keep the tanker off the bar, but this only increased the vessel's list and trim dangerously. When some of Sybert's crew heard that a motor lifeboat from Chatham was on the way on their personal radios, efforts to maneuver the stern were stopped.

As the *CG-36500* approached Chatham's bar, Webber and his crew began to sing Rock of Ages and Harbor Lights. Their voices were soon muffled by the thunderous roar of the ocean as it collided with the sand bar.

116

As the *CG-36500* crossed the bar, the boat was smashed by a mountain of a wave and thrown high in the air. The boat landed on its side between waves. The self-righting boat recovered quickly and was smote again, this time tons of seawater crashed over the boat breaking its windshield and flattening coxswain Webber.

Quickly scampering to his feet, Webber noticed the boat's compass had been knocked off its mount. The cold, near hurricane force winds howled through the boat's cockpit as Webber

U.S. Coast Guard MLB to the rescue

struggled to regain control and steer in to the towering waves.

The *Pendleton's* engineer and his crew sensed their demise as the stern hulk hobby-horsed southward smashing bottom with each new series of waves. Although there were several Coast Guard cutters and the *CG-36383* nearby, the fortunes of fate would only allow *CG-36500* and her crew alone one attempt to save engineer Sybert's men. Coxswain Webber finally brought *CG-36500* across the bar and knew the water was deeper because the spacing between the waves had increased and so had the wave heights. Weather observations from nearby cutters involved in the *Fort Mercer* and *Pendleton* rescues indicated sea heights between 40 to 60 feet.

Occasionally, the lifeboat's engine would die out when the waves would roll the vessel so far over that the gasoline engine would lose its prime. Each time, engineer Fitzgerald would crawl into the cramped compartment to restart the main engine --- his efforts were rewarded with severe burns, bruises, the steady chug-chugging of the engine and the collective sighs of appreciation from his shipmates.

The boat proceeded roller coaster fashion as it slowly labored up one side of a huge wave and surfed down the backside, accelerating towards the trough. Coxswain Webber knew too much speed was not good and unchecked, would cause the boat's bow to bury in the next wave and swamp the small vessel. The boat's motion was so swift, coxswain Webber had to reverse the engine on the backside of each wave in order to slow it down. His first navigational waypoint was the nearby Pollock Rip Lightship, where Webber hoped to reorient himself and give his crew a breather in the lee of the larger vessel.

The weather and visibility worsened in freezing horizontal snow that lashed the coxswain's face through the broken windshield. He wore no lifejacket in order to give himself the best chance to react and guide the vessel. After about an hour of struggling and fearing he had missed the lightship, coxswain Webber slowed the *CG-36500* to a near standstill as he sensed, rather than saw,

Winter storm at sea

something ahead. He sent a crewman forward to energize the boat's small searchlight. Within seconds, the light was on and a large wave lifted this crewman up and over the coxswain flat and carried him aft where he landed onboard, miraculously unhurt, with a thud.

Creeping the boat forward, the searchlight soon revealed a pitch black mass of twisted metal, which heaved high in the air upon the massive waves and then settled back down in a "frothing mass of foam." Each movement of the giant hulk produced a cacophony of eerie groans as the broken ship twisted and strained in the 60-foot seas. No lights were apparent as coxswain Webber maneuvered the small boat aft along the port side of the Pendleton's stern section.

Rounding the stern, *CG-36500's* searchlight illuminated the word *PENDELTON* and moments later, the larger vessel's own deck lights became apparent. And, then a small figure above began frantically waving his arms! He soon disappeared. Coxswain Webber then saw a mass of people begin to line *Pendleton's* starboard stern area, many shouting muffled instruction, which were unintelligible over the wind and crashing seas. He looked upon their position as "inviting" relative to his own and thought of strategies for he and his crew to join them above.

Without notice, a Jacob's ladder was tossed over the side, and unbelievably, men began to start down the ladder like a procession of ants! The first man at the bottom was dunked in

Mural at USCG Academy by Tony Falcone depicting rescue of seaman from the "Pendletonon" February 18, 1952. Dedicated by Class of 1962 in September 2005

the water like a tea bag and then lifted 50 feet in the air as the *Pendleton* rolled and heaved. Webber sent his crew forward to assist.

Coxswain Webber skillfully maneuvered the *CG-36500* along the *Pendleton's* starboard quarter and, one by one, the *Pendleton* survivors either jumped and crashed hard on the tiny boat's bow or fell in to the sea, where Webber's crew assisted them onboard at great personal risk. Some *Pendleton* crewmen were sling-shotted out from the ship on the Jacob's ladder by the whipping and rolling motion of the

119

waves. As soon as they had reached their zenith of flight, the ship would snap roll them back violently and slam them against the side of the *Pendleton.*

After multiple approaches and 20 survivors safely recovered, the *CG-36500* began to handle sluggishly. The human parade continued to descend unabated. There was no turning back as coxswain Webber arrived at yet another defining moment and made the decision that they would all live or they all would die.

And, so it went as Webber and his crew literally stuffed their human cargo aboard and risked life and limb again and again. Finally, with 32 survivors onboard the *CG-36500* there only remained the 300-pound giant of a man George (Tiny) Myers, the inspiration of the *Pendleton* crew for his

Painting commissioned by the U.S.C.G. to commemorate the most famous sea rescue in Coast Guard history

personal heroics, suspended at the bottom of the ladder. Myers had distinguished himself by his unselfish attitude in helping the other 32 crewmen before considering his own situation.

Myers jumped too soon and was swallowed up by the sea. Moments later, he was again visible underneath the stern of the vessel, clinging to one of *Pendleton's* 11-foot-long propeller blades. Easing ahead cautiously, Webber felt the stern of the small boat rise as a monstrous wave overtook *CG-36500.* The boat was driven ahead faster and faster towards Myers. Coxswain Webber backed his small craft's engine hard, but the boat smashed into *Pendleton* and Tiny Myers. The *CG-36500* was ejected from underneath the *Pendleton* by another large wave just as the hulk was lifted one last time and rolled over and sank.

All was again dark as the *CG-36500's* searchlight was extinguished. Coxswain Webber was sick at the thought of losing Tiny Myers, but knew the fate of the 36 men on his small boat rested exclusively in his hands. Lost with no compass to steer by and in zero visibility conditions, there were just two choices. Head east into the seas and hope to survive 10-12 more hours until a new

Thirty two men rescued from the sinking Pendleton

day's light brought the slim chance of transferring passengers yet again to a larger rescue ship. Or, put the wind and seas on the small boat's stern and let them force the vessel ashore someplace where help might be nearby.

Coxswain Webber then tried his radio again and received an immediate acknowledgement. Once he briefed his superior that he had 32 *Pendleton* survivors aboard, there ensued a squabble between the nearby CG cutter *McCulloch* and the Chatham Lifeboat Station about various options. These included a suggestion of an at-sea rendezvous with *McCulloch* and a second transfer of survivors! The radio was quickly turned off and Webber devised a plan to beach the *CG-36500* at first opportunity. The small vessel would be held on the beach as long as possible with the engine while the survivors clambered ashore. On cue, the *Pendleton* crew gave a cheer of approval and support and on they went.

121

Very soon, a red flashing light appeared! And, the boat's searchlight incredibly revealed the buoy that marked the turn to the entrance to Old Harbor, Chatham and safe water!

A quick call to the station was met with excitement and elation for now everyone knew that the rescued were now survivors! Soon, another stream of over-direction and gibberish caused coxswain Webber to secure the radio after requesting assistance with the survivors at the fish pier.

The event made headlines all over the world

A crowd of Chatham men, women and children met the *CG-36500* at the pier, securing lines and helping the shocked, excited and in some cases, sobbing survivors and rescuers ashore.

In a message to the Chatham Lifeboat Station the day after the rescue, Rear Admiral H. G. Bradbury, Commander of the First CG District, sent his personal congratulations to BM1 Webber and his crew for their "outstanding seamanship and utter disregard of your own safety in crossing the hazardous waters of Chatham bar in mountainous seas extreme darkness and falling snow during a violent winter gale to rescue from imminent death thirty two crewmembers... minutes before the tanker capsized."

In all, 24 Coast Guardsmen were honored for their efforts during the Fort Mercer-Pendelton rescues. Seventy of the possible 84 crewmen were eventually saved from the broken vessels.

3 Lost in Wellfleet Wreck - '59

The Body of *Paulmino's* Captain found

Once more the seas have claimed and have yielded up the dead.

The body of Captain Angelo Marino of Richfield Avenue, Everett, skipper and owner of the 83 foot Boston dragger, Paulmino, was found on the beach at South Wellfleet early Sunday morning. The fishing vessel foundered on a bar near Cohoun's Hollow during a wild storm last Thursday night.

Six members of the crew attempted to swim to shore through the pounding surf, two of whom, Charles Piazza, 27, of Boston, the cook, and Joseph Panto, 32, also of Boston, perished in the attempt. Their bodies were recovered. Four who survived the ordeal are James E. Clements, Jr., of Somerville; John Norris, 39; Michael Ciarmetaro, 42, , and Frank Ciarmentaro, all three were from Gloucester. All are recuperating in good condition at Brighton Marine Hospital, Boston.

Trapped by Waves

Mr. Clements told the Coast Guard that Captain Marino had been trapped aboard the boat by huge waves, as the others made their desperate attempt to reach shore. Mrs. Laurrel Cardinal of Wellfleet, who lives a few hundred feet from the scene of the wreck, also told Coast Guardsmen she had witnessed Captain Marino's attempts to escape.

"I saw him swept over the side by a huge wave, and then saw him crawl back into the bow of the boat," she said.

The Captain's body was found by two Chatham Coast Guardsmen, Engineman 3rd Class Frank Sheeley and Seaman Apprentice Robert Smith of the Chatham Station. They were patrolling the shoreline, part of a series of patrols which had been maintained since the vessel was wrecked. Captain Marino's trousers and wallet had been found on Friday, three quarters of a mile from the scene of the wreck

Provincetown Advocate 9 Apr 1959

The General Greene - 1960

The rescuer was rescued

She was built in 1927 and stationed at Boston, Massachusetts. In 1941, off the coast of Greenland, she located and rescued 39 survivors of the torpedoed freighter SS *Marconi*.

In May 1942 she responded to a call for assistance from the torpedoed British freighter SS *Peisander* off Nantucket Shoals. *General Greene's* lookout sighted a U-boat crash diving dead ahead

The

Driven onto the beach while on a rescue mission

General Greene acquired the U-boat on sonar and dropped three depth charges onto the sub producing an oil slick some 400 feet in diameter. The cutter then returned to the SS *Peisander's* lifeboat and rescued the ship's 18 survivors.

On 7 March 1960, she grounded at East Sandwich while on a rescue mission during the height of a fierce Nor'easter. Her tow line became entangled in her propellers, rendering her engines useless. Though both her anchors were quickly dropped, only the port anchor kept the cutter from grounding immediately.

The cutter Acushnet responded but had to stand off due to the heavy winds and 40-foot seas. After the *General Greene* lost her starboard anchor and chain, the power of the winds and seas that finally drove her onto the beach. It took four days for the cutter *Acushnet* from seaside and the Massachusetts National Guard working from the beachside, to refloat the *General Greene*.

Eldia – 1984

The *Eldia* was blown ashore in East Orleans, Massachusetts on March 29, 1984 and was refloated two months later. A year later the ship was scrapped.

After delivery of its load of Colombian sugar in Saint John, New Brunswick the *Eldia* was hit by a storm delivering 80-mile-per-hour winds. This storm was part of a period of extreme weather which caused President Ronald Reagan to pledge federal disaster relief.

Spectators on the beach

Her captain, Ernesto Garces, was hampered by her lack of contemporary electronic technology for monitoring the weather, which had enabled other ships in the area to anticipate the problems that would come with the storm and take appropriate action.

All he could do was monitor radio broadcasts. He attempted to bring the ship under control but was forced onto Nauset Beach at around 4pm. Two hours later the ship was abandoned by its crew of 23 Filipinos, who were rescued by a helicopter from Air Station Cape Cod.

Due to the ease of access to the area New England residents crowded to see the sight when the weather improved. One estimate is that more than 150,000 did so. The town collected $81,693 by charging $2 a day for visitors' car parking, and many businesses conducted a lot of additional trade during this curious period.

The wreck was drawn back off the beach on May 17, 1984, taken to a scrap-yard in Rhode Island and then on to another at Staten Island. The ship was reportedly cut up in 1985.

U.S.S. Constitution visits Harwich

A high point in the maritime history of Harwich was the visit of the *U.S.S. Constitution* on October 24, 1882

October 24. 1882, the streets of Harwich Port were enlivened by the sailors and officers of the Frigate *Constitution* and the Steam Frigate, *Powhatten*. "Old Ironsides" had been towed to Harwich Port, where they were both anchored. To be sure, people from all the villages of Harwich and the surrounding Towns flocked to the waterside to see the famous vessel. This may have been especially true because the Harwich Independent said that this would probably be her last trip.

She was out of commission and on her way to Portsmouth, New Hampshire, to be broken up and scuttled.

However, the Constitution continued to rise like the Phoenix. Restoration took place between 1925 and 1927. Further, major

U.S. Constitution under sail

restoration was completed in 1996 for the 200th anniversary of "*Old Ironsides*" in 1997, when she again went under sail.

The *U.S.S. Constitution* was launched in 1797, displacing 2,200 tons. She was built of oak, cedar and hard pine. Bolts, which fastened her timbers and the copper sheathing on the bottom of her hull, were made by Paul Revere. She generally carried more than 50 guns and a crew of 450 men.

She was engaged in heroic service to our country in the War of 1812. She defeated disabled and captured the British frigate, *Guerriere*, and then, destroyed and caused to surrender, the British frigate, *Java*. She was christened, "*Old Ironsides*", by her crew, because British shot failed to penetrate her oaken hull, which was little damaged in her battles.

Wrecked Harwich Vessels, 1872-1900

As chronicled by THE HARWICH INDEPENDENT

ELVIRA J. FRENCH

The *Elvira J. French* was a four-masted schooner that was launched at the shipyard of William Adams and Son, East Boothbay, Maine, on August 26, 1890. She had a (7) beam and the length of her keel was 179 feet. She weighed 902 tons net. She was the largest ship that had been built in East Boothbay for 40 years and the first four-master ever built there.

One of the owners of the *French* was Theophilus B. Baker of Harwich Port. Better known as "T.B.", Captain Baker attended Pine Grove Seminary from 1847 to 1852. The *Elvira J. French* was christened by Kate Florence Baker, the Captain's daughter, for whom his earlier vessel, the *Kate Florence*, had been named.

Elvira J. French under construction in East Boothbay

In addition to her beauty the *French* could boast of her speed. In March of 1891, she sailed New York to Brunswick, Georgia, a distance of about 725 miles, in just four days. In 1895, she ran by Point Judith, Rhode Island, only 31 hours after leaving Philadelphia.

In June of 1894, Captain Baker commanded his own vessel on a trip to Philadelphia. By 1896, Captain Lewis B. Doane, of Harwich Port, had become skipper of the *Elvira J. French*. In 1897, with Captain Josiah Newcomb in command, the *French* ran into a storm in the Atlantic, shortly after leaving Gibraltar. She sprang a leak, and then, ran out of coal to fuel her steam pumps. The crew turned to hand pumps to keep her afloat, and fortunately, she was able to make port safely at Gloucester.

Captain Sears Linwood Moore of East Harwich, popularly referred to as T. Linwood", assumed command in 1899. The record shows him to be Master as the *Elvira J. French* sails from Philadelphia to Boston that year.

In 1901, the *French* encountered a severe storm on her way from Mobile to New York. She lay in a crippled condition at the Delaware Breakwater. However, she was repaired and returned to service. Finally, the *Elvira J. French* met her end on September 15, 1904, a victim of the *"Portland Gale"*. She foundered at sea, seven of her crew perished and only two were saved.

FLEETWING

Research shows that the name *"Fleetwing"* has some prominence in the Maritime History of Harwich. On March 4, 1884, the British Brig, *Fleetwing,* being piloted by Captain Isaiah Cahoon of Harwich, parted her chains off South Harwich and went ashore near Harding Beach. The crew was rescued but the vessel was a total loss.

Some years later, in the obituary of Captain Uriel Doane of West Harwich, the name *"Fleetwing"* appears once again. This time, *"Fleetwing"* refers to a command that Captain Doane held in his earlier days as a Sea Captain. While word of this vessel is very limited, it seems unlikely that the relationship of the two *"Fleetwings"* is anything more than the coincidence of the name and its connection with Harwich Seamen!

FLORENCE NORWELL

November 10. 1891: The Schooner *Florence Norwell*, with a Captain Nickerson in command sank off Pollock Rip during the October Gale. Reports-have circulated that the *Norwell* was in the company of the Schooner *Hattie Crowell* on the Evening of October 22nd. Both were lost.

FRANK LUCAS

The Harwich Schooner, *Frank Lucas*, under the command of Captain James 0. Hulse was bound for Roatan, Honduras from Mobile, with lumber. The Schooner was wrecked off Central America. on April 28, 1877, according to a report dated May 24, 1877. While the crew was saved but the vessel and cargo were total losses. The *Frank Lucas* was 50 tons, built at Philadelphia in 1858.

GENERAL LYON

On December 1, 1874, it was reported that the *General Lyon* was for sale. Interested parties were directed to Captain Ivory B. Kelley, Harwich Center, or, Captain Coleman Kelley, Harwich Port. The same notice ran again on January 7, 1875. Later, on May 2, 1877, Captain Ivory Kelley was listed as the Master of the General Lyon, as the Schooner sailed for the fishing grounds.

In 1878, with Captain Abner R. Woodhouse in command, the Schooner *General Lyon* made no less than ten departures/returns to Harwich Port. At each return to T.B. Bakers Wharf between 170 and 280 barrels of mackerel were unloaded. The Schooner would be in port no more than two or three days before beginning another trip to the fishing grounds. The *Lyon* was hauled-up for the winter on October 23, 1878.

On March 27, 1879, the *General Lyon* arrived, at Harwich Port, from New Bedford fit for another season of mackereling. She sailed south on April 8, 1879 with Captain Kelley in command. The Schooner would do fourteen trips from Harwich Port in 1879. She would off-load over one thousand barrels of mackerel between April and early November, when she was hauled for the season. Captain Isaiah Cahoon brought the *General Lyon* into Harwich Port on March 24,

1880 to begin the season. As in other years, the *Lyon* sailed in and out of Harwich Port until May 1st, when the following report appeared:

"T.B. Baker's Schooner General Lyon, under Captain Isaiah Cahoon arrived in Harwich Port, Saturday, with the loss of a seine boat. He had been cruising five weeks without seeing a sign of mackerel, feeling discouraged. Spoke, to a Bark last Thursday, which reported mackerel fifteen miles out. Found plenty of mackerel off Bamagat, W. by N., forty-five miles out. The General Lyon had taken fifteen, barrels when a blow came on and interrupted the catch and carried away the seine boat, so returned home."

Ship on Fire

October 26, 1880, "A cry of fire ran through the village of Harwich Port"! It was discovered that: "The *General Lyon*, lying off back the bar, was on fire in her cabin. W.B. Kelley and the owner, T.B. Baker, with the assistance of Lewis B. Doane, E.H. Taylor, John T. Allen, J.L. Clark, J.D. Allen and Joshua Burgess took a boat and started for the burning ship. Her cabin, quarter deck, and mainsail all burned. The crew lost all their clothing and everything connected to the voyage.

Captain Baker's loss is $3,000, insured for $1,000. Captain Isaiah Kelley was Master of the ill-fated vessel. She was twenty years old and had taken one thousand one hundred barrels of mackerel this season.

GEORGE L. TREADWELL

It was reported, on November 25, 1875, that Captain George Taylor of Harwich had left Town for New York to take control of the Schooner *George L. Treadwell.* The next and final report of the *Treadwell,* August 9, 1877, indicates that the Schooner is bottom-up near Burmuda after capsizing in a gale. The Schooner was formerly owned by Captain George Taylor.

HATTIE N. GOVE

The Schooner *Hattie N. Gove*, of Harwich Port, under Captain Baxter D. Kelley, Jr., ran ashore on Falmouth Flats, on the night of November 3, 1887. She was pulled off without

Squall downs sailing ship

apparent damage by the *U. S. Revenue Cutter Gallatin* and towed to Vineyard Haven. A dispatch, on January 17, 1888, from Savannah, reported that the Schooner *Hattie N. Gove*, with Captain B.D. Kelley, Jr., in command, had struck a shoal off Port Royal Bar. The Schooner and cargo were a total loss. Captain Watson N. Small served as Mate. The Schooner carried a cargo of guano.

HELEN A.

The *Helen A.* was a 27 foot catboat built by Flavius Nickerson. He sold it to James Chase of Dennisport to be used for-fishing. On Her maiden voyage, in June of 1887, she capsized on the way to Edgartown

HELEN M. CROSBY

In a report dated October 23, 1883, the plight of the Schooner *Helen M. Crosby* is vividly described. Captain Orick Higgins of Harwich was in command , when a sudden squall came out of the Northeast, as the *Crosby* and some 200 other vessels were fishing in Cape Cod Bay. Captain Higgins lost eight members of his crew, three of whom were Harwich men. Captain Ivory Kelley of Harwich Centre, aged 50 years was identified as one of the Harwich men to perish.

ISLAND CITY

The story of the Harwich Schooner, *Island City*, begins with the sighting of a *sea Serpent*. While fishing off Nauset Light, at around 2 pm, October 22, 1875, Captain Edward B. Allen noticed an object in the distance that kept appearing

Spotted a Sea Serpent

and disappearing. At first, the Captain thought it was a boat but later he decided it must be a sea serpent.

The Schooner's Log for October 22, 1875 shows that a sea serpent had been seen off Nauset Light.

From 1875 to 1897, the *Island City* had no less than six Captains: Edward B. Allen, twice; Abisha Doane; Amos Kelley; Edwin Studley; Leomard Studley; and, Elias Chase.

In February, 1876, the *Island City* had a narrow escape. She went ashore off Harwich Port, in a storm. The crew and those on shore thought the vessel would be a total loss. Fortunately, she survived and had many more productive fishing years.

The *Island City* belonged to the Harwich mackerel fleet, along with the other Schooners *Albert Steele, Nettie Moore* and *Little Lizzie*. Records show that the *Island City* made frequent trips to New York to deliver fish. From May of 1877 to September of that year, she made four trips to New York. En route, the Schooner often went through the dangerous waters of the Heligate.

On Her last trip for 1877, in September, the *Island City* left Harwich Port, bound for New York. She first sailed to Beverly and upon entering the harbor, Captain Allen misjudged his location and ran into a bridge, breaking the Schooner's martingale.

J. LINDSAY

In November, 1875, Captain William Tuttle of Harwich Port, and Captain of the Monomoy Life Saving Station. bravely rescued the crew of the *J. Lindsay*, which was ashore on Shovelful Shoal. The Boston press spoke in the highest terms of the bravery of Captain Tuttle.

JAMES HOYT

In early February, 1893, Captain Theodore Ellis of West Harwich went to Boston to take command of the 3 masted Schooner *James Hoyt*. He proceeded to Norfolk, Virginia. Later, the Schooner parted her chain during a gale near the Bass River.

She drifted ashore at South Harwich near the mouth of Red River. She was driven so far ashore that she came to rest in the shade of a pine tree. Ice encircled the *James Hoyt* and extended as far as a mile off shore. Chatham wreckers

Ship similar to the Julia A. Brown

began the work to float Her for $350.

JULIA A. BROWN

The large and splendid three-masted Barque *Julia. A. Brown* was launched at East Boston on November 27, 1873. She was built under the inspection of Captain Edgar Paine, agent for the American Lloyds Company. She is classed "Al" for eleven years. Her model has been called superior by most competent judges and was built of the best materials by Messrs. Campbell and Brooks. The length of keel is 135 feet; breadth of beam is 34 feet; depth of hold is 9 feet; and, depth of decks is 6 feet. She is owned by Messrs. Kilham, Land & Co., Nathaniel Brown, P.A. Nickerson and others. She is under the command of Captain Joshua Nickerson of Harwich Port.

The report of January 22, 1874, describes a quick passage for the new Barque between Boston and Charleston Bar of just five days. As their report states, "with Captain Nickerson in command, She was deeply laden".

The next report, on April 13, 1880, announced the arrival of the *Brown* at New York after an absence of three years, Further, the report states that Captain Dennis Nickerson, who has been in charge over those three years will be replaced by Captain Joshua Nickerson for the *Brown's* next voyage.

By March of 1882, Captain Dennis S. Nickerson is back in command. After stopping at Harwich Port on the 8th, inst., the *Julia A. Brown* went on to Boston.

The report of January 19, 1886, is ominous, to say the least. The Barque *Julia A. Brown*, with Captain Dennis Nickerson in command, cleared Perth Amboy, NJ, January 6th, for Boston. She probably ran aground on Handkerchief Shoals. Wreckage washed ashore at Chatham and at Harwich Port.

Wreck lies on the bottom

The final report about the Barque is dated February 2, 1886, and, states very simply that a search party cruising "...the Bar has been unsuccessful in locating the *Julia A. Brown*.

LIZZIE PHILLIPS

The fishing Schooner *Lizzie Phillips* parted Her mooring off Deep Hole, South Harwich, on September 30, 1889. She was completely wrecked on the Dennis Shore.

MARY DOANE

The *Mary Doane* was owned by Captain Valentine Doane, Sr. of Harwich Port. While his mother and sister were both named "Mary", it is uncertain for whom the vessel was named.

The first report of the *Mary Doane* was in November, 1872. She was furnished with a new main mast and main topmast before proceeding to the West Indies to engage in the fruit trade. However, from 1873 to 1883, the record indicates that the *Mary Doane* was engaged in mackereling and made many trips to the Banks. While most of these trips were successful. July of 1878, She reported seeing many mackerel, "but they wouldn't take the hooks"!

The *Mary Doane* had her share of close calls with the weather and the sea. In June of 1874, she went aground at West Chop. Fortunately, She came off without damage. In April, 1881, the *Mary Doane* was caught in a gale 100 miles off Cape Henry. She lost her seine, her seine boat and her dory. Her bulwarks and headgear were carried away. Two sailors, James Baker and Isaiah Prince, were aloft for 30 minutes, while the vessel was riding under bare poles. Again, She rode out the storm.

Though there were plenty of mackerel in the area, the Schooner was powerless to take them in the storm.

Schooner in trouble

In the early years, Captain William Taylor was in charge, followed by: Captain Whitemore, 1877; Captain Kelley and Captain Nickerson, 1878; and Captain Chase in 1879. In May of 1883, the last report of the *Mary Doane* tells of her parting her chain in a gale. She dragged ashore near the mouth of the Herring River. Because she had but one anchor and 30 fathoms of chain, crew members aboard were unable to save her.

NETTIE MOORE

The *Nettie Moore* was launched in 1876 in Essex. She displaced 155 tons, and was built to engage in mackerel fishing. Her principal owner was Captain Levi Eldridge, of South Chatham.

The *Nettie Moore* was named for the daughter of a part owner of the vessel, Captain Sears L. Moore of East Harwich, who also served as Her first Commander. The Schooner was expected to be "high line". It was projected that She would become the leading vessel in the fishing fleet in regard to profit. In 1877, Her stock was $12,000 and the prediction came true!

In April, 1878, the *Nettie Moore* arrived in New York with the year's first landing, some 25,000 mackerel. In June, She went to Chaleur Bay-between.New Brunswick and the Gaspe Peninsula.

By July, the *Moore* had landed 150 barrels of fish; by the 12th of that month, the total on board was up to 250 barrels. In August, She shipped home from Canada some 350 barrels of mackerel, and, on August 24, 1878, the *Nettie Moore* arrived at South Harwich with an additional 350 barrels. All in all, she had landed a total of 700 barrels—truly, high line!!

Sailors abandon sinking ship

In June of 1879, the Schooner's fortune turned. Captain Moore and members of the crew, including E. Steadman Eldridge, came down with a fever from an unknown illness. The Captain was compelled to give up his command.

Three years later, he had still not completely recovered from the mysterious disease. Captain Frank Cahoon, the husband of Nettie Moore, for whom the Schooner had been named, succeeded Captain Moore as Master.

Misfortune continued to plague the *Nettie Moore*. Early in 1880, the vessel ran ashore in Vineyard Sound and missed most of the fishing season. Finally, on May 3, 1881, while returning to Harwich with a sick crew member, She ran onto

Sow and Pigs Ledge and "bilged". The crew took to the boats. The *Nettie Moore* was a total loss

PHEBE J. WOODRUFF

Built in 1882 by Jacob Fuller of Booth Bay, Maine, the *Phebe J. Woodruff* was a three-masted, center-board schooner. She was owned by Captain Theophilus B. Baker of Harwich Port. Her specifications were: 140' keel; 35' beam; 13' depth of hold; 90' mainmast; 52' topmast; 62' spanker boom; and, 26' bowsprit. The sails were made by S.B. Kelley and Son of Harwich Port and contained 3,500 yards of canvas. Charles Jenkins, also of Harwich Port, made two boats for the *Woodruff*, one at 21`, the other 16'.

The *P.J. Woodruff* had many "modem" conveniences for both officers and crew. Several Harwich Seamen served on the *Woodruff*: Joseph E. Berry was first mate; second mate, Albert C. Wixon; and Luther K. Snow served as steward.

For her ten years of operation, the- *Phebe J. Woodruff* went mackereling as well as making several trips caning Coal, ice and other cargo from Maine to Florida. She did not always enjoy good fortune. The *Woodruff* was in several disasters in heavy gales, collisions and strandings on sand bars, which required frequent extensive and expensive repairs!

Over the years, Captain Baker shared command of the *Phebe J. Woodruff* with other Harwich Captains. Captain Elisha Mayo, who was part owner, served until 1885, when he sold his interest in the *Woodruff*. Next, Captain Benjamin Kendrick was in command, serving into 1889. For a brief time, in 1888, Captain Kendrick was relieved by Captain Crowell Nickerson, but returned to command in October of that year. Capt. Baker appears to have resumed command in July of 1889. Captain Will Watts commanded the Schooner from January, 1891, to November of 1892.

Ship's Suicide

The news account of November 29, 1892 would be the final word about the *Woodruff*. Under Captain Will Watts, the *Woodruffs* demise is referred to, as the "Ship's Suicide". One of her own spars, in being carried away in a gale off New

Jersey, pierced her hull causing her to sink. All aboard were rescued by the schooner *Jennie S. Hall*. Excluding her cargo of coal, the *Phebe J. Woodruff* was valued at $22,000

R.S. SPOFFORD

In January of 1895, the following reports appeared regarding the Schooner *R.S. Spofford*:

January 1. 1895: The Schooner *R.S. Spofford* was lost last week on the North Carolina Coast. The Steward, Sylvanus Chase of Harwich did not survive;

January 15. 1885: The family of Sylvanus Chase have the satisfaction of knowing that his body was recovered and he was given a proper burial;

January 22. 1885: Extensive report of the death of Sylvanus Chase indicates that being unable to hold on any longer, Mr. Chase went to sleep and froze to death.

Sails ripped from the mast

ROBERT PETTIS

The Harwich Schooner *Robert Pettis* foundered in Narragansett Bay, December 14, 1874. All aboard were from Harwich and. lost their lives in the sinking of the *Pettis*. In addition to the Captain, Sidney Ellis, the following men were lost: Henry Cobb Hendren, George Andrews, James B. Ellis (Captain's nephew), and the cook, Ezra Smith

S.B. FRANKLIN

On October 27, 1891, it was learned that the Schooner *S.B. Franklin*, owned by Femandus G. Kelley of Dennisport, and commanded by Captain Frederick Kelley of North 'Harwich, had gone ashore at Duxbury and went to pieces within an hour.

The dead body of Captain Kelley was found on board, but no crew were found. They evidently took to the boats and perished. The Captain's sons, Frederick, Jr., and, James C. were lost. In addition, Captain Kelley left his wife, daughter and four brothers. Another brother, Ivory, had been lost in about the same place some years ago

Ships Sunk by
German U–Boats

German torpedo strikes cargo ship

Ships Sunk by German U-Boats off Cape Cod

Ship	Date Sank
Tug "Perth Amboy" + 4 barges	July 21, 1918
Cruiser	August 3, 1918
Dornfontein, Trawler	August 3, 1918
Aleda May	August 3, 1918
Rob Roy	August 3, 1918
Sydland	August 8, 1918
Sidney Atwood, Trawler	August 10, 1918
Mary E Bennett	August 10. 1918
Earl and Nettie	August 10, 1918
Anita Perry, Trawler	August 10, 1918
Progress	August 10, 1918
Reliance	August 10, 1918
William H Starbuck	August 10, 1918
Old Time	August 10, 1918
Adair	January 1942
Robin Hood	April 16, 1942
Norwegian Taborfjell	April 30, 1942
Port Nicholson	June 6, 1942
Cherokee	June 6, 1942
SS Pan-Pennsylvania	April 15, 1944

German Attack on Cape Cod!

"ORLEANS, MASS., July 21. - An enemy submarine attacked a tow off the easternmost point of Cape Cod today, sank three barges, set a fourth and their tug on fire and dropped four shells on the mainland." [Dallas Morning News, 21 July, 1918]

When most people think of Cape Cod, they think of sandy (or rocky) beaches, windswept expanses of dune grass, Henry David Thoreau, the Kennedys, and for the summer of 2012, sharks. But on July 21st, 1918, the town of Orleans, on the outer portion of the Cape's "elbow," became the site of the only attack on US soil by the German Empire during World War I. This incident was the first time since the War of 1812 that the territorial United States had been directly attacked by a hostile force.

A German U-Boat fires on shipping

At approximately 11 o'clock in the morning, the German U-Boat *SM U-156* surfaced about 2 miles off Nauset Beach, the easternmost point of Cape Cod. It commenced firing at the American tug boat *Perth Amboy* and the four barges that the tug was towing from Gloucester, Massachusetts to New York City. Upon sighting the vessel , Captain J. H. Tapley of the tug immediately sounded a warning and ordered the four barges abandoned. Under heavy shelling, the *Perth Amboy* and its barges were set afire. Three of the barges sank, fortunately giving the 41 crew and passengers sufficient time to board lifeboats and escape to shore.

The attack continued for about an hour, during which a crowd of thousands of Cape Cod residents were drawn to the area by the sound of the U-Boat's guns. According to a news piece on the incident by the *Bellingham Herald* of Washington State,

"The flashes of the guns and the outline of the U-Boat were plainly seen. Danger was not thought of until a shell whirled over their heads and splashed in a pond a mile inland. Three other shells buried themselves in the sand of the beach." [The Bellingham Herald, 22 July 1918]

Ten miles to the north, meanwhile, the Chatham aviation station had responded to the attack by deploying two hydroplanes, armed with depth charges. The appearance of

Germany U-boast similar to one which shelled Orleans in 1918

these craft caused the U-Boat to briefly break off its attack and submerge, only to resurface when the planes once again flew north towards Chatham. This time, when the planes turned around and began to fly low as if in preparation for an attack, the German vessel disappeared under the waves and was not seen again.

Damage from the raid was estimated to be in the range of $90,000 for the destroyed barges and $100,000 for the *Perth Amboy*. Torpedoes, shells and other ordinance fired by the U-Boat was estimated to have cost the German Empire the equivalent of $15,000. There was general confusion as to why the submarine would have gone to the trouble of navigating the treacherous shoals of Cape Cod just to waste ammunition on small craft. The opinion of the United States government was that the Germans were attempting to shake American morale by targeting American soil, and that Orleans, in the extreme east of Cape Cod, was just in an exposed position.

Others have suggested that *SM U-156* had been stalking a larger collier that had passed by on its way to New York just days before, and that the *Perth Amboy* just happened to be in the wrong place at the wrong time.

All accounts seem to agree that the attack could have been much worse than it was. No American warships were around at the time of the raid, leaving the U-Boat free to do as much damage as possible. Despite their free reign, the Germans were unable to sink all of the barges and succeeded only in damaging the tug without managing to completely destroy her. None of the crew were killed, nor were several women and children whom who were aboard, although one sailor had his arm blown off.

Although several shells were aimed at the town of Orleans, one landed in a pond and three others buried themselves harmlessly in the sand. Accounts of the attack describe the Germans taking half an hour to hit and sink one of the smaller barges. This was derided by American newspapers as poor shooting but could also suggest outdated or malfunctioning equipment.

U.S. Government Assumes Control of the Cape Cod Canal

Sobered by this close call, the American Navy began to improve the defenses of the First Naval District in New England. Ships began to sweep the waters off of Massachusetts. To shorten shipping routes and protect other coal convoys, the Federal government assumed control of the Cape Cod Canal, providing direct access to Buzzard's Bay and the Atlantic Ocean from Cape Cod Bay. The busy port of Boston remained open, but merchant ships were warned of the risk before setting course for open waters.

SM U-156 managed to escape undetected, although rumors persisted amongst the residents of the coastal Northeast that pursuing American warships had been heard and even sighted engaging the U-Boat. The submarine is believed to have sunk after striking a mine in the North Atlantic in September of 1918, several months after its assault on Cape Cod.

The children of Orleans, quick to capitalize on the event, set up a table overlooking Nauset Beach. On the table was a cage with a sheet over it, and in the cage was a chicken. For ten cents, gawkers at the beach could lift the sheet and behold the "chicken that survived the sub attack."

Cape Cod Times - July 21, 1918

Men from the nearby Coast Guard station rushed up to the observation tower to see what the commotion was. One of them called Chatham Naval Air Station to inform them of the ongoing U-boat attack. Reuben Hopkins, a Coast Guard veteran of the engagement, reached the tower rail in time to see an enemy shell explode over the tugboat. The *U-156* then started firing upon the barges. Escaping from the now burning *Perth Amboy* and barges were 32 merchant sailors and civilians, including the captain's wife and children.

Reuben Hopkins stayed behind as other men went to rescue the tugboat survivors who were coming ashore in lifeboats. Soon, Curtiss HS-2L and R-9 seaplanes arrived to bomb the U-boat, but the ordnance dropped either were duds or failed to hit the target and the warplanes had to fly back to Chatham, Massachusetts to reload.

SM U-156 got away and headed North, where it continued to attack other allied ships. Back in Orleans, a few shells and craters were found on shore; some also were found in the nearby marsh. The area sustained minor damage. The psychological effects on the population of Orleans were immediate as people began reporting the hearing of naval battles off the coast.

Adair Sunk - 1942

Went Down With a Cargo of Gold Bullion

In the last week of January 1942, the *Adair* sailed with a cargo of spare aircraft parts, other military supplies, and $30,000 in gold bullion ($32 an ounce at the time), meant to finance American troops purchase of goods in Iceland. She sailed east to clear Long Island, and then headed north for Newfoundland. Her captain and crew were unaware that a German submarine, the U-123, was waiting.

Meanwhile, Hardegen, captain of the U-123, brought his submarine to the surface off the coast of Massachusetts. The *Adair* was clearly silhouetted against the lights dogging the coastline, and the Germans spotted her. Hardegen tracked the *Adair* for 30 minutes before he brought his sub to bear on her.

He fired a single torpedo that exploded directly beneath the *Adair*s hull, snapping her cleanly in half. Flames from the exploding ship lit the sky for miles, and the *U-123* quickly submerged and retreated southward. Within minutes the *Adair* sank, with all hands, in deep water off Cape Cod, taking the bullion and her officers and crew down with her.

Cherokee - 1942

Passenger Ship Torpedoed, 85 Perish

On June 6, 1942, the German submarine *U-87* fired a spread of two torpedoes at the leading ship of convoy XB-25, the *Cherokee*, off of Cape Cod during a gale

The *Cherokee* was struck by one torpedo on the port side under the bridge. The explosion lifted the vessel out of the water, destroyed the chart house and incoming water gave the ship a sharp list to port.

The speed was increased and the rudder was turned hard right, but a second torpedo

The Cherokee

struck the port bow 90 seconds later, causing the ship to sink by the bow with a 60 degrees list to port within six minutes.

The rough seas and the extreme list prevented the launching of lifeboats and only seven rafts were cut loose. The ship carried nine officers, 103 crew men, 11 armed guards (the ship was armed with one 4in, two .50cal and two .30cal guns) and 46 US Army passengers. Three officers, 62 crew men, one armed guard and 20 passengers died. 44 survivors were picked up by the American steam merchant *Norlago* and taken to Provincetown, Massachusetts the same day. 39 others were picked up by *USCGC Escanaba* (WPG 77) which took them to Boston.

Port Nicholson - 1942

Struck by Two Torpedoes

The Port Nicholson was in the same convoy as the passenger ship Cherokee. The first torpedo fires from the German sub *U-87* hit in the engine room where two crew members on watch below were killed, the second torpedo hit aft and caused her to settle by the stern, while *HMCS Nanaimo* took

Port Nicholson

off the master, 80 crew members and four gunners.

At dawn, the ship was still afloat and it was decided to re board her to assess the damage and chances of salvage. The boarding party consisted of the master, the chief engineer and one officer and three ratings from the corvette. After they had boarded the vessel, wind came up and the rough seas broke the weakened bulkheads causing her to sink quickly by the stern.

The men climbed down the ladders and got into the lifeboat but the suction of the sinking ship overturned the lifeboat, drowning the master, the chief engineer, the officer and one rating. The surviving two men from the boarding party were picked up by the corvette, which then brought the survivors to Boston, Massachusetts.

Wreck Located Off Cape Cod with <u>$3 Billion</u> in Platinum, Silver and Gold Aboard

PORTLAND, Maine (AP) - Greg Brooks, co-manager of Sub Sea Research, hopes to recover treasure of platinum, silver and gold from the British merchant ship Port Nicholson.

The Port Nicholson, carrying 1,707,000 troy ounces of platinum, and four other ships were being escorted by six military ships in a convoy from Halifax to New York in 1942.

German sub U-87 breaking water

The Port Nicholson was sunk by the German U-boat *U-87* along with a cargo of 71 tons of platinum now worth a reported $3 billion.

"I'm going to get it, one way or another, even if I have to lift the ship out of the water," Brooks said.

Brooks said the Port Nicholson was headed for New York with 71 tons of platinum valued at the time at about $53 million when it was sunk in an attack that left six people dead. The platinum was a payment from the Soviet Union to the U.S. for war supplies, Brooks said. The vessel was also carrying gold bullion and diamonds, he said.

Brooks said he located the wreck in 2008 using shipboard sonar but held off

Platinum bars

announcing the find while he and his business partners obtained salvage rights from a federal judge. According to SSR research, the Port Nicholson and four other ships were being escorted by six military ships in a convoy from Halifax to New York. Brooks has recovered several identifying and critical artifacts. He has verified that "it is without a doubt the Port Nicholson".

Late in the summer of 2011, after 100's of hours of ROV video, they have seen what appear to be bullion boxes containing 4 bars, each being 400 troy ounces of precious metal. "We have seen boxes indicative of those used to store and ship this type of bullion in 1942. Our video clearly shows the box and our inspection class remotely operated vehicles (ROV) could not lift it due to its weight of about 130 lbs."

During World War II the availability of platinum was limited since it was declared as a strategic material. Use of platinum for most non-military applications was prohibited. After the war, consumption of platinum increased due to its catalytic properties.

Cargo Ship "Robin Hood" - 1942

April 16, 1942, the unescorted and unarmed Robin Hood was hit on the starboard side by two torpedoes from the German submarine *U-575* while steaming on a zigzag course at 11 knots in rough seas southeast of Nantucket Island, Massachusetts.

The ship had been missed five hours earlier by a first torpedo. One torpedo struck amidships at the fire room, killing one officer and two crewmen on watch below and caused a boiler explosion that lifted the deck up and folded it over.

The next hit forward of the first and blew the hatch covers off the #1 and #2 holds and carried away the foremast. The vessel flooded rapidly, broke in two at #3 hatch and sank within seven minutes. The most of the nine officers and 29 crewmen aboard abandoned ship in one lifeboat, but other three officers and eight more crewmen were lost. The survivors were picked up on 23 April by *USS Greer* (DD 145) and landed at Hamilton, Bermuda.

Cargo Ship Taborfjell - 1942

April 30, 1942, the unescorted Norwegian cargo ship Taborfjell was hit by two torpedoes from the German sub *U-576* in waters East of Cape Cod and caused the ship to

Taborfjell

sink within one minute. The ship sank so quickly that no lifeboats could be launched and the three survivors of her twenty man crew had jumped overboard and rescued themselves on a raft. They observed how the U-boat had seen three other survivors but passed them without taking any action.

SS Pan-Pennsylvania - 1944

World's Largest Tanker Sunk by U-boat off Cape

Pan-Pennsylvania sailed from New York Harbor on the afternoon of April 15, 1944 as part of convoy CU-21, bound for England, carrying 140,000 barrels of 80-octane aviation fuel, a crew of 50 men, and 31 members of the Naval Armed Guard. The 28 merchant ships of CU-21 were accompanied by

SS Pan-Pennsylvania – largest tanker in the world

Escort Flotilla 21.5, which consisted of six destroyer escorts.

Weather conditions were initially poor, and the convoy was not able to settle into the standard convoy formation until the next morning. However, they had already been observed by the German submarine *U-550* which, under the command of *Kapitanleutnant* Klaus Hanert, was on her first combat patrol. At 8 a.m. SS *Pan-Pennsylvania* was straggling behind the rest of the convoy when she was hit by a torpedo from *U-550* on her port side.

As *Pan-Pennsylvania* began to settle, the *U-550* approached her, using the stricken ship to mask their presence from the three escort destroyers — *Joyce*, *Peterson* and *Gandy* — who rapidly approached, scanning the area with their sonar. Aboard *Pan-Pennsylvania* a fire broke out in the engine room, and the captain ordered the crew to abandon ship, as she began to settle and list to port. The crew launched two lifeboats and three life-rafts as water began to wash over the deck. The tanker continued to settle and then slowly capsized.

U-550, meanwhile, attempted to slip away, but was detected by *Joyce*, which promptly attacked with a pattern of 13 depth charges, bracketing the submarine and forcing her to the surface. The three escorts opened fire on her and *Gandy* rammed her abaft the conning tower. *Peterson* fired two more depth charges from her "K" guns, which exploded alongside the submarine. *U-550* attempted to man her deck gun and machine guns, but the crews were mown down by gunfire. The crew of *U-550* then set scuttling charges and attempted to abandon her, but the charges exploded prematurely and she quickly sank taking most of the crew with her. The entire action, from the detection of *U-550* to the time her sinking, lasted only thirteen minutes.

USCG Destroyer Escort Joyce

Of the crew of *Pan-Pennsylvania*, 31 were rescued by *Joyce* and 25 by *Peterson*, leaving 25 unaccounted for. Only 12 Germans survived, including her Captain, 44 were lost.

On the day following the attack an attempt was made to sink the still burning hulk of *Pan-Pennsylvania* with gunfire. This failed, so she was bombed and sunk by aircraft the day after. The wreck of *U-550* was found on July 23, 2012, in deep water about 70 miles East of Cape Cod.

German Submarine *U-550* - 1944

Sank *SS Pan Pennsylvania*, Sunk by USCG – Grizzly Postscript

A Type IX C-40 U-boat under the command of Kapitänleutnant Klaus Hänert, departed on her first patrol on 6 February 1944. She sailed from Kiel for the North Atlantic and conducted weather reporting duties before sailing for Newfoundland and later the northeast coast of the United States. On 16 April, she located convoy CU-21, bound for Great Britain from New York. The tanker SS *Pan Pennsylvania*, the largest tanker in the world, was unwisely straggling behind the convoy and the *U-550* torpedoed her. The tanker quickly caught fire and began to sink. As the tanker settled, the submerged U-boat sailed underneath her in an effort to hide from the inevitable counteract by the convoy's escorts.

Germans on the conning tower of their sinking sub awaiting rescue by USCG SS Joyce as the Pan-Pennsylvania burns on the horizon

Convoy CU-21 was escorted by Escort Division 22, consisting of Coast Guard-manned destroyer escorts reinforced by one Navy DE, the USS *Gandy*, which took the place of the USS *Leopold*, which had been lost in action the previous month. The escort division's flagship, USS *Joyce* and the USS

Peterson rescued the tanker's surviving crew, and then the *Joyce* detected the U-boat on sonar as the Germans attempted to escape after hiding beneath the sinking tanker.

The *U-550's* engineering officer later said, "We waited for your ship to leave; soon we could hear nothing so we thought the escort vessels had gone; but as soon as we started to move-- bang!" The *Joyce* delivered a depth-charge pattern that bracketed the submerged submarine. The depth charges were so well placed, a German reported, that one actually bounced off the U-boat's deck before it exploded.

The attack severely damaged the *U-550* and forced the

U-550 Sinks as USS Joyce comes alongside for survivors

Germans to surface, where they manned and began firing their deck guns. The *Joyce*, *Peterson*, and a Navy destroyer escort, the USS *Gandy*, returned their fire. The *Gandy* then rammed it abaft the conning tower, and the *Peterson* dropped two depth charges which exploded near the U-boat's hull. Realizing they had little chance, the U-boat's crew prepared scuttling charges and abandoned their submarine.

The *Joyce* rescued 13, one of whom later died from wounds received during the fire-fight. The remainder of the U-boatmen went down with their submarine. *Joyce* delivered

156

the prisoners of war and the *Pan Pennsylvania* survivors to the authorities in Great Britain.

There is a grisly postscript to the sinking of the U-550. According to the Eastern Sea Frontier's War Diary account of the sinking of the U-550, some of the crew actually survived the sinking and were trapped in a forward compartment of the U-boat.

The survivors apparently attempted to escape from the U-boat as it lay on the ocean floor using their escape lungs. At 1515 on 5 May 1944, the Coastal Picket Patrol *CGR 3082* recovered a body from the sea in 39° 51' North x 71° 58' West, about 93 miles ESE of Ambrose. The body was clothed in a German-type life jacket. From the markings on his clothing it was possible that the man's name was "Hube." A German escape lung was found near his body as well. An autopsy performed on the body indicated that the individual died only five days before his body was discovered -- the *U-550* had been sunk on 16 April and the body was found 19 days later.

Two other bodies were subsequently found. The first, picked up by another picket boat, *CGR-1989*, at 1730 on 11 May, was fully clothed, had an escape lung and life jacket on. He was found in a rubber raft. Identification marks indicated the man was a German sailor named Wilhelm Flade, age about 17. The body was transferred from *CGR-1989* to *CGR 1338* on the morning of 12 May 1944 and was brought to Tompkinsville.

On 16 May a third body was sighted and picked up by *USS SC-630*. It was stated that the uniform and insignia indicated the victim had been a German crewman, although he carried no identification; that he had been in the water more than 18 days.

Secret Nazi Super Sub Found

Why has the existence of this ship been kept secret for seventy years?

June, 1993 - Massachusetts treasure hunter finds remains of a WWII Nazi submarine. They soon realized that this was not a typical U-boat for it was twice as large as any Nazi sub ever seen.

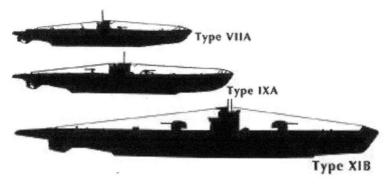

"Black Knight's" size compared to other U-Boats

Time and much research would suggest that their find was the legendary Super Sub known by several names; "Schwartz Ritter" or Black Knight, Hitler's Escape Sub, XI U-Cruiser and, *U-112*. It was a Type XI-B U-boat that plans for the construction of which were reportedly scuttled in 1939.

The ship's dimensions are impressive: length 377 feet, beam 31 feet, height 40 feet and a range of 15,800 miles. She would have a crew of 110 men plus two companies of "Special Forces Troops." A company can consist of anywhere between 80 to 200 men therefore suggesting the XI-B could transport 160 to 400 persons in addition to her officers and crew. Her cargo capacity was reported as 600 cubic tons above provisions.

It was found off the easterly shore of Cape Cod shore buried in the Cape's shifting sands in sixty feet of water. Sixty feet is two atmospheres deep and within reach by scuba divers without major concern about de-compression and the "bends." The treasure hunters reportedly made several dives to the sub and recovered scores of artifacts. Visibility was low and the currents strong making their survey of the boat difficult.

Does or did the XI-B really exist?

There are those who say no

German records show that construction of four XI-B class (Long distance) submarines were commissioned to be built at the shipyards at Bremen in September of 1939. However, the construction was "officially" cancelled four month later. Four XI-B keels had been laid by that time.

> **All official histories claim the vessel**
> **type XI-B was never built.**

Others suggest yes

However, there are hints that at least one vessel of this type was indeed launched from the Deschimag yards. Contained within the records of the military archive at Freiburgim-Breisgau, Germany is a brief mention of the "actual" yard trials in the Weser River of the Type XI U-Cruiser having attained a surface speed of 26 knots. This is supported to some degree in Eberhard Roessler's publication "The U-Boat", in which this trial record is partly quoted.

Is this the "Black Knight" on the bottom off the Cape?

The details contained in the records of the military archive in Germany make it very clear that the above speed trials were not obtained from 'tank' tests of models.

Therefore, there certainly is some proof of the actual existence of a working and operational model of the legendary Type XI.

Finnish Intelligence report refers to a "Hitler Escape Boat" being readied for transport in 1944.

Reports obtained from interviewed veterans of both the Allied and Axis intelligence services indicate very strongly that in early 1944 there was a Type XI berthed at a port on the Iberian Peninsula. These same sources have stated that the unofficial reference to the Type XI was *"Der Schwarz Ritter"* (*"The Black Knight"*) - perhaps the very same *Black Knight* as is reported to lay in the sand off Cape Cod on Orion Shoal.

Why the secrecy?

Most of the clandestine activity directed by the Germans toward the Americas originated through a German Industrial-Intelligence organization referred to as "Sofindus" also based on the Iberian Peninsula. Sofindus served as the

German gold ready for transport

Nazis' commercial agency in Spain, handling all non-military trade and developing Spain's mining and agricultural industries, principally to supply the Third Reich with raw materials vital for its economy and war industries.

By 1944 it was painfully apparent to many in Germany that it was only a matter of time before the Allies won the war.

160

Two German Special Operations known as "Jolle", (translated as "Happy Boat") and "Aktion Feuerland", (meaning "Action Land-of-Fire", referring to Argentina), were set up designed to pave the way for German post-war survival.

Sofindus, Nazi leaders, industrialists and bankers were co-operating in laying the financial foundation for a "Fourth Reich" within the borders of Argentina and other South American countries.

Submarines would make ideal transports to carry the influential Germans and their wealth to Argentina. They are said to have nicknamed the XI-B sub "Hitler's Escape Sub" in order to explain the activity and attention the ship was receiving.

Establish a 4ᵗʰ Reich in Argentina

The conversion of paper money into hard assets such as gold, silver and jewels had been accelerating along with the inflation Germany was experiencing. Inflation was accelerating at a frantic pace as Germany's defeat was becoming more apparent.

The huge capacity of the XI-B could carry several hundred influential persons plus billions in gold within its expansive hull. The 15,000 mile range of the sub meant they could travel from Europe to Argentina non-stop without re-fueling.

Coincidence?

On July 20ᵗʰ 1944 two, perhaps related, events occurred. The first, and extensively reported, was the failed assassination attempt on Adolph Hitler's life by the Nazi Opposition.

The second, on the same day, was the un-noticed sailing of the *Black Knight*. Thirty seven days later the U-Boat was spotted off the Massachusetts coast by a Pan Am airplane.

Two U-Boats tracked approaching America

British Admiralty, "ULTRA," notifies U.S. Office of Naval Intelligence of an unknown U-boat heading their way,

Headlines of July 20. 1944

perhaps they are the "Special Operations" known as "Jolle", and "Aktion Feuerland". They are traveling together on parallel courses under radio silence and not reporting their positions daily as was the usual U-boat protocol.

U. S. Navy located and was tracking German U-boat *U-1229* but was unaware of a second U-boat or its location. They sank the *U-1229* just east of the Grand Banks.

Black Knight reached a point about seven miles east of Great Point, Nantucket and surfaced the evening of 25th to send a diplomatic message in a "High Priority" status. The captain was unaware that he had been spotted by the Pan-Am plane and considered it safe to surface.

What the U-boat captain did not know was that three ships and a Naval Airship, K-25, were already headed in his direction.

The telegraph operator at Chatham forwarded the coded message to the Cryptographic Center in Washington and from there to White House Map Room. The Map Room was actually the Intelligence Center for combined services and managed by Department of State.

Black Knight sends a Secret Message to the White House and is Sunk by Naval Airship

There were reportedly only two de-coding machines in the world able to decode the XI-B's message, the one in Washington (provided by German collaborators), and the other in Berlin.

Shortly after the XI-B's sending of the mysterious message, the Naval Airship K-25 from South Weymouth Naval Air Station arrived upon the scene and dropped two depth charges onto the sub. One was a dud but the other hit just aft of the conning tower blowing a large hole in the hull as the sub dove beneath the surface.

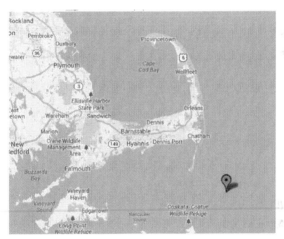

Reportedly the location of the sunken XI-B on Orion Shoal

There are no "official" records of the sinking of the XI-B yet veteran interviews have revealed that naval vessels conducted a 48 hour surface search for survivors and debris. The search was conducted at exactly the same location where the wreckage of the Type XI-B was discovered in 1993.

Official Records

August 25, 1944

- Cape Cod Radio Intercept Telegrapher intercepts and re-transmits a diplomatic "B-Bar" U-Boat transmission emanating from a point close to Chatham, MA.
- Naval Airship "K-25" encounters U-Boat submerging 14 miles southeast of Chatham and sinks it with one attack on Orion Shoal.
- Washington Attack Log shows an unknown U-Boat's transmission early in the evening stating "Being attacked by aircraft."
- Eastern Sea Frontier Northern Group Command authorizes a U-Boat search within the area of Orion Shoal off Cape Cod.

August 26, 1944

- Airship "K-27" on "Special Search" to Orion Shoal
- Meeting at Chatham with listening station personnel – "Events of August 25th never happened"
- Debriefing of K-25 crew – "Events of August 25th never happened"
  K-25's pilot is reported to have remarked – "Yes, damit! I sank the sub and I want credit for it." He is said to have been transferred to South America the very next day.

Last heard from the sub's discoverer:

- Neither German nor American officials will discuss anything to do with the XI-B with us.
- Navy has positioned 4 sono-bouys around the wreck and this is creating havoc with our magnetic survey and side scan sonar.
- ***"We are experiencing serious security issues. . ."***

German *U-123* Captain Honored in 2012

Germany's last surviving U-Boat captain who helped sink dozens of U.S. and British ships has been honored by the Germany's military in his homeland seven decades after he was twice decorated by Hitler for bravery.

Reinhard Hardegen, 99, was one of the most successful commanders during "Operation Drumbeat" sinking 27 Allied ships along the east coast of North America.

The first seven months of 1942 were nicknamed by German commanders as the 'American Shooting Season'.

The 1898 Portland Gale

Hundreds of ships
and lives lost
all along the
New England Coast

PORTLAND

Steamer PORTLAND - Nov 1898

THE PORTLAND SUNK; 118 LIVES LOST.

STEAMER FROM BOSTON WRECKED SUNDAY OFF CAPE COD WENT DOWN IN THE STORM. THIRTY-FOUR BODIES OF PASSENGERS SO FAR RECOVERED.

NEWS TAKEN TO BOSTON BY A SPECIAL COURIER, TELEGRAPHIC COMMUNICATION BEING IMPOSSIBLE.

Boston, Mass., Nov. 29. -- The steamer *Portland*, bound from Boston to Portland, went down off Truro, on the outside of Cape Cod, Sunday morning. Every man, woman, and child on board at the time of the disaster was drowned, in all 118.

NONE LIVES TO TELL.

The *Portland* left Boston on Saturday evening and was last seen afloat by a fisherman in the vicinity of Thacher's Island several hours later. Nobody knows what happened in the awful hours on the angry sea which followed, and the lips that might tell the tale are sealed in death.

Steamer Portland

The surmise is that with the wind blowing a gale at the rate of seventy miles an hour, a rate which has never been equaled except once before in the written history of weather along this coast, with the waves running to mighty heights, the steamer became disabled and was swept by the raging seas across the entrance to Massachusetts Bay and down upon the "Graveyard of Cape Cod".

The *Portland*, with its side paddlewheels and large exposure of hull, must have been smashed by the seas and rolled by the mad waves, and at last foundered in the height of the gale Sunday morning.

The news of the disaster is meager because of blockaded railroads and fallen telegraph wires. The only additional facts brought from Cape Cod by a courier, who was thirty-two hours making the journey, is that vast quantities of wreckage of the Portland and thirty-four bodies have been cast upon the beach at Truro.

The first discovery of the disaster was made by Surfman Bowley of the High Head Life Saving station, who found on the beach the body of a negro encircled by a life belt of the steamer *Portland*. Soon after bodies were washed ashore and recovered by the life-saving crews of the three stations in the vicinity. Not a glimpse of the steamer was obtained by the life savers. The destruction of the vessel was complete, as hundreds of barrels, boxes, and other

articles of freight attest. From just east of the Peaked Hill Bar Station to the High Head Station, three miles eastward, the shore is heaped with debris.

The *Portland* carried a miscellaneous cargo of 100 tons of merchandise.

The vessel was built in Bath, ME in 1890, and was a side-wheel steamer of 1,517 tons net burden. Her length is 230 feet, beam 42, depth 15 feet. She was valued at $250,000 and is fully insured.

WRECKAGE 15 MILES SOUTH

Dr. Maurice Richardson of Beacon Street, this city, has been at his summer home at Wellfleet during the storm, and his story corroborates the early accounts of the loss of the *Portland*, for he saw two of the bodies washed ashore and on them were life preservers marked with the vessel's name. Dr. Richardson was on the first train from Cape Cod which arrived in this city late to-night. To take the train he was obliged to ride fifteen miles.

"I saw two of the bodies picked up," said Dr. Richardson. "One was probably that of a deckhand, a man of about twenty. He had on a life preserver marked '*PORTLAND.*' The other body was that of a stout woman. She, too, wore a life belt with the steamer's name on it.

WRECKAGE WHICH CAME ASHORE AFTER THE STEAMER PORTLAND WAS LOST AND LIFE PRESERVER FROM THE ILL-FATED CRAFT.

Life preserver in right foreground.

Wreckage is coming ashore for fifteen miles along the coast. I picked up three piano keys and a piano cage ashore, but, of course, I do not know that they were from the *Portland*. Among the wreckage was a large quantity of furniture upholstered in red plush. Then there were cased of lard directed to *Portland*."

"I was fifteen miles south of High Head. There is nothing in the fact that wreckage was found so far south to contradict the report that it was at High Head that the *Portland* struck, for the current runs south along the shore."

Dr. Richardson said he had heard one theory advanced that the *Portland* had foundered far to the north, somewhere near Cape Ann, and that all the wreckage and bodies had drifted across the bay to Cape Cod. He said that at Orleans the body of a girl of about twenty was found. She had a gold watch and a ring marked "J.G.E." Her watch stopped at 9:17. The double wheel of the *Portland* came ashore at Orleans.

The insurance upon the hull of the *Portland* was placed in Boston, partly in the Boston Marine Insurance Company and partly through the Boston office of Johnson & Higgins. It was valued at about $200,000. The insurance upon the cargo of the steamer, which consisted of dry goods, boots and shoes, flour, &c., was placed in New York and amounted to $45,000.

The New York Times New York 1898-11-30

Spreading the News - Orleans to France to New York to Boston

The storm severed telegraph and electric lines knocking out all communications in the area making it difficult to get news of the *Portland* to Boston. The problem was solved by sending a wire to France over the trans-Atlantic French cable from the station in Orleans. From there the news was wired back to New York over another cable and then telegraphed to Boston.

Damage widespread

Calling the damage widespread is a vast understatement. Houses were blown over and washed away all along the coast from Cape Cod to Portland, Maine. The coastline was littered with the wrecks and wreckage of dozens of vessels, large and small, smashed or sunk by the fierce winds and seas.

In Provincetown harbor alone over 30 vessels were blown ashore or sunk. Damage along Boston's south shore and Cape Cod was probably the worst; telegraph lines were brought down, railways washed out, and even the low scrub trees of Cape Cod were blown away. In Scituate, a small coastal community 30 miles south of Boston, the coastline was permanently altered when mountainous waves cut a new inlet from the sea to the North River, closed the old river mouth, and reversed the flow of part of the river.

Timeline chronicling the storm

Portland departed Boston for the final time at 7 PM on November 26, 1898, crowded with passengers returning home after the Thanksgiving holiday. At the time of her departure the weather was worsening, but had not yet deteriorated to the point that sailing was deemed inadvisable. As she steamed northeast towards Portland, however, conditions quickly worsened. At 9:30 PM she was sighted passing Thatcher's Island, a short distance northeast of Boston, her progress clearly hampered by the deteriorating weather. Although she was still making headway against the storm at this sighting, she probably did not get far before her progress was stopped.

Between 11 and 11:45 PM *Portland* was sighted three times, but this time to the southeast of Thatcher's Island - she was being driven south by the storm. When sighted at 11:45 PM, she is said to have shown severe storm damage, especially to the superstructure. By this time conditions on the steamer must have been dreadful, and all aboard must have known they were in grave danger. Unable to make progress against the storm and unable to make for safe port, *Portland*'s only hope lay in working her way offshore and riding out the storm at sea. Her attempts to reach the open sea accounted for her slow movement to the east between the 9:30 and 11:45 sightings.

At 5:45 AM the following morning, lifesavers on Cape Cod heard four blasts of a steamer's whistle. It is now believed the whistle was that of the doomed *Portland*. In the course of the night the storm had driven her even further backwards, so

172

she was now far southeast of Boston. Between 9:00 and 10:30 that morning the eye of the storm passed over, and several persons claim to have seen *Portland* wallowing five to eight miles offshore, clearly in great peril. No further sightings were made that day, as the storm closed in once again.

At 7:30 that night, more than 24 hours after *Portland* had sailed, a lifesaver on his regular beach patrol found one of the steamer's lifebelts washed up on the beach. Fifteen minutes later several forty-quart dairy cans were found in the surf. At 9:30 doors and woodwork from *Portland* were found. Around 11:00 the rising tide brought in massive quantities of wreckage, giving clear evidence that *Portland* had been lost. It is said that this tragic news was communicated to the world via a bizarre relay - by telegraph across the trans-Atlantic cable to France, then to New York via another undersea cable, and from there on to Boston - for the telegraph cables between Cape Cod and Boston had been blown away by the storm.

All those aboard *Portland*, believed to be a total of 191 passengers and crew (the only passenger list was lost with the ship), were killed. Eventually 36 bodies were recovered along the beaches.

Many of the bodies wore wristwatches that had stopped at 9:15. It is unclear; however, if this indicates the ship was lost at 9:15 AM, or at 9:15 PM. Although there are several reports of the ship being sighted, afloat, between 9 AM and 10:30 AM that day, the exact times of those sightings are not known. If any of those sightings took place after 9:15 AM, then the ship must have survived until 9:15 PM that day, some 26 hours and 15 minutes after she had started her doomed voyage.

However, *Portland* would not have carried enough fuel to remain at sea, in storm conditions, for over 24 hours. She could have burned furnishings, interior bulkheads, and other wooden materials to keep the boilers running, but the quantity of this material washed ashore tends to indicate this action was not taken. Also, it is highly questionable whether she could have held together for 24 hours, given the terrible sea conditions. Still, the fact that major debris did not begin to wash ashore until 9:30 PM suggests that *Portland* had survived into the night - surely, if she had been wrecked at

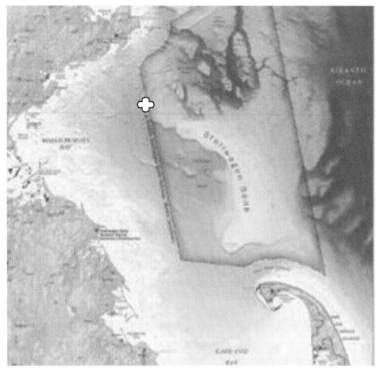

9:15 AM, debris would have been washed ashore in the morning. Because the exact time of the final sightings cannot be firmly established, it is impossible to conclusively determine the exact time of *Portland*'s loss - either 9:15 AM, or 9:15 PM, on Sunday, November 27, 1898.

Ship Found off Stellwagen Bank

Portland's remains were eventually located on the seafloor about seven miles offshore, and have since been explored. The small schooner *Addie E. Snow* was also lost during the storm, and her remains lie less than 1/4 mile from *Portland*'s grave. It is thought that the two vessels may have collided, hastening their ends.

Portland lies in 460 ft of water off Stellwagon Bank

Vessels Lost or Damaged in the Portland Gale

New England Vessels Caught in the Storm

Name Of Vessel (Type), Life-Saving Station / Homeport / Captain/Crew / Nature Of Casualty

- A.B. Nickerson (whaling schooner), Cape Cod
- A.B. Nickerson (steamer), Cape Cod
- Abby K. Bentley (schooner), Vineyard Sound / Providence
- Abel E. Babcock (schooner), Boston Bay / Capt. Abel E. Babcock/8 ~ *Sometime during the evening of November 26-27 she came to anchor in an exceedingly dangerous place, made unavoidable to circumstances, and dragged onto Toddy Rocks nearly 1 mile from shore, NW of Hull, MA. She was pounded to fragments and all on board perished.*
- Addie E. Snow, Cape Cod
- Addie Sawyer (schooner), Vineyard Sound / Calais, ME
- Adelaide T. Hither (sloop), Plain, NY ~ *Blown well up on the beach in Fort Pond Bay. Master requested assistance from keeper to float her, and station crew went over and locked her up ready for launching.*

Ship's remains in the sand

- Africa, Portland, ME
- Agnes, Cape Cod
- Agnes May, Cape Ann
- Agnes Smith, Pt. Judith, RI
- Albert H. Harding (schooner), Boston Bay / Boston, MA
- Albert L. Butler (schooner), Peaked Hill Bars, MA / Boston, MA / Frank A. Leland/7 ~ *Two crewmen and*

one passenger were lost on November 27 when she wrecked high onto a beach near the Peaked Hill Bars Station.

- Alida (schooner), White Head, ME ~ *While lying in Islesboro, gale sprang up, parting her anchor chains and driving her to sea. Blown along for some 20 miles, finally fetching up on the flats at Lobster Cove. Crew reached shore without difficulty.*
- Aloha (schooner), New Shoreham, RI
- Amelia G. Ireland (schooner), Gay Head, MA / NY NY / Capt. Oscar A. Knapp ~ *After she stranded in Menemsha Bight, her crew tried to lower her boat, but it was carried away leaving them without means of escape. They also tried to float a line ashore. The only life lost was a mate who perished in the rigging.*

Ship Aground, Crew in the Sea

- Anna Pitcher (schooner), New Shoreham, RI / Newport, RI
- Anna W. Barker (schooner), White Head, ME / Sedgwick, ME ~ *Wrecked on Southern Island, 3 miles from station. Crew escaped without injury.*
- Annie Lee, Cape Ann
- Arabell (schooner), Block Island, RI / Newport, RI
- B.R. Woodside (schooner), Boston Bay / Bath, ME
- Barge (unknown), Boston Bay
- Barge (unknown), Boston Bay
- Barge (unknown), Boston Bay
- Barge (unknown), Boston Bay
- Barge (unknown), Boston Bay
- Barge (unknown), Cape Ann

- Beaver (sloop), Vineyard Sound / Wilmington, DE
- Bertha A. Gross, Cape Ann
- Bertha E. Glover (schooner), Vineyard Sound / Rockland, ME
- Brunhilde (sloop), Point of Woods, NY
- Byssus, Vineyard Sound
- C.A. White (schooner), Boston Bay / Fall River, MA
- C.B. Kennard, Boston Bay
- Calvin F. Baker (schooner), Point Allerton, MA / Dennis, MA / 8 ~ *About 3:00 a.m. on November 27, in the midst of the storm with some of her sails blown away, she stranded on the northerly side of Little Brewster Island. She pounded in and fetched up about 75 yards from the rocks. All hands were driven to the rigging as the breakers swept over the ship. The schooner became a total wreck and three men were lost.*

Schooner H H Chamberlain

- Canaria, Vineyard Sound
- Carita, Vineyard Sound
- Carrie C. Miles, Portland, ME
- Carrie L. Payson (schooner), Chatham, MA ~ *Stranded 1 mile N. of the station.*
- Cassina, New Shoreham, RI
- Cathie C. Berry (schooner), Vineyard Sound / Eastport, ME
- Champion (brig), Quoddy Head, ME / 6 ~ *Wrecked near the Quoddy Head station, but her crew succeeded in reaching shore in their own boat.*
- Charles E. Raymond (schooner), Vineyard Sound / Dennis, MA

- Charles E. Schmidt (schooner), Cape Ann / Bridgeton, NJ
- Charles J. Willard (schooner), Quoddy Head, ME / Portland, ME ~ *While lying at anchor in West Quoddy Bay, a gale sprang up and her chains parted. She soon stranded and her crew was helped by life-savers and local fishermen.*

Schooner on the beach

- Chilion, Cape Ann (schooner) / Portsmouth, NH
- Chiswick, Boston Bay
- Clara Leavitt (schooner), Gay Head, MA / Portland, ME / 7 ~ *Stranded the morning of November 27 and didn't last an hour. Breakers swept over her heavily as the crew took to the rigging. Her deck house was destroyed in 20 minutes and all three masts fell when the weather shrouds slackened. Six lives were lost.*
- Clara Sayward, Cape Cod
- Clara P. Sewall, Boston Bay
- Coal Barge No. 1, Point Allerton, RI / 5 ~ *Wrecked near Toddy Rocks. A line was fired across the vessel, but the crew was too nearly exhausted to be able to do anything with it. The vessel was rapidly breaking up as the life savers fastened lines around their bodies and waded out into the surf to rescue them. All were so chilled that they had to be carried to a nearby house.*
- Coal Barge No. 4, Point Allerton, MA / Baltimore, MD / 5 ~ *Struck on Toddy Rocks between 12-1:00 a.m. November 27 and went to pieces so quickly that assistance would have been impossible. Of the 5 on board, only the captain and one sailor managed to reach the shore alive by clinging to a piece of the deck house.*

- Columbia (pilot schooner), Scituate, MA / 5 ~ *She was sighted near Boston Lightship around dusk, lying becalmed. Then the storm struck, and she apparently put about in an attempt to get offshore to ride out the storm. This attempt failed and she had no choice but to anchor. Both anchor chains parted, and she broke up on Cedar Point. Her entire crew was lost and only three bodies were recovered.*
- Consolidated Coal Barge No. 1, Boston Bay
- Daniel L.Tenney, Boston Bay
- David Boone, Cape Cod

Mertis H. Perry

- David Faust (schooner), Nantucket / Ellsworth, ME
- Delaware, Boston Bay
- D.T. Pachin (schooner), Cape Ann / Castine, ME
- E.G. Willard (schooner), Vineyard Sound/ Rockland, ME
- E.J. Hamilton (schooner), Vineyard Sound / NY NY
- Earl (cat), Cuttyhunk, MA
- Edith (cat), Cuttyhunk, MA
- Edgar S. Foster (schooner), Brant Rock, MA / 8 ~ *Wrecked near Brant Rock. Crew succeeded in reaching shore unaided and went to a vacant cottage.*
- Edith McIntire, Vineyard Sound
- Edna & Etta (schooner), Great Egg, NJ / Somers Point, NJ ~ *Stranded on the meadows during the storm. Master asked for help from the station and the crew boarded the vessel. At high water they put rollers under her and hove her afloat.*
- Edward H. Smeed (schooner), New Shoreham, RI
- Ella F. Crowell, Boston Bay
- Ella Frances (schooner), Cape Cod / Rockland, ME
- Ellen Jones, Cape Cod
- Ellis P. Rogers (schooner), Cape Ann / Bath, ME
- Elmer Randall, Boston Bay
- Emma, Boston Bay

- Ethel F. Merriam (schooner), Cape Cod / Booth Bay, ME
- Evelyn, Cape Ann
- F.H. Smith (schooner), Cape Cod / New Haven, ME
- F.R. Walker (schooner), Cape Cod / Gloucester, MA
- Fairfax (steamer), Cuttyhunk, MA ~ *During the gale and snowstorm, she brought up on the Bow and Pigs ledge, about 3 miles to the W. of the station but was not immediately discovered by the patrol on account of thick weather. Her master stated crew and passengers didn't wish to leave until they could be transferred to a tug. After dinner, a tug being seen on the way to the stranded vessel, surfmen close-reefed sail and stood down to lend a hand in assisting with the transfer of passengers, crew and baggage to the tug which then proceeded to New Bedford.*

Juanita

- Falcon, Vineyard Sound
- Fannie Hall, Portsmouth, NH
- Fannie May, Rockland, ME
- Flying Cloud, Cape Ann
- Forest Maid (schooner), Portsmouth, NH / Portland, ME
- Fred A. Emerson (downeast lumberman), Boston Bay
- Friend (steamer), Cuttyhunk, MA / Boston, MA
- Fritz Oaks, Boston Bay
- G.M. Hopkins (schooner), Boston Bay / Provincetown, MA
- G.W. Danielson (steamer), New Shoreham, RI
- Gatherer, Cape Ann
- George A. Chaffee, Cape Ann
- George H. Miles, Vineyard Sound
- Georgietta (schooner), White Head, ME ~ *Stranded on Spruce Head Island during the heavy gale and snowstorm. In attempting to haul her off, the foremast and main topmast were carried away.*

- Grace (schooner), Cape Cod / Ellsworth, ME
- Gracie, Cape Cod
- Hattie A. Butler (schooner), Vineyard Sound / Hartford, CT
- Henry R. Tilton (schooner), Point Allerton, MA / 8 ~ *Parted chains during the hurricane and stranded near the station. All members of the crew landed without accident. The sea was very heavy and at times washed over the sea wall, submerging the surfmen and their apparatus.*
- Ida, Boston Bay
- Ida G. Broere (cat), Lone Hill, NY / Patchogue, NY ~ *Parted moorings during the gale and went ashore 1/2 mil from the station on the bay side. Surfmen could do nothing for her on account of sea and ice until December 4.*
- Idella Small (schooner), Davis Neck, MA / Portland, ME / 3 ~ *Driven ashore by the gale on the east side of Davis Neck. As she took bottom one of her crew jumped ashore and sought help at the station. Two others on board safely off. On the next high tide after she went ashore, the vessel drifted up on the beach at Bay View and became a total wreck.*

Henry R Tilton

- Inez Hatch, Cape Cod
- Institution (launch), Boston Bay
- Ira and Abbie (schooner), Block Island, RI / New London, CT
- Ira Kilburn, Portsmouth, NH
- Isaac Collins (schooner), Cape Cod / Provincetown, MA
- Island City, Vineyard Sound

182

- Ivy Bell (schooner), Jerrys Point, NH / Damariscotta, ME/ 4 ~ *Dragged ashore near the entrance to Portsmouth Harbor. All crewmen taken off safely.*
- J.C. Mahoney (schooner), Cape Ann / Baltimore, MD
- J.M. Eaton (schooner), Cape Ann / Gloucester, ME
- James A. Brown (schooner), Vineyard Sound / Thomaston, ME
- James Ponder (schooner), Vineyard Sound / Wilmington, DE
- James Webster, Boston Bay
- John Harvey (barge), Pt. Judith, RI / NY NY

Sailing Ship on the bottom

- John J. Hill, Boston Bay
- John S. Ames (schooner), Boston Bay
- Jordon L. Mott (schooner), Wood End, MA / Rockland, ME / Capt. Dyer/5 ~ *One life lost when she sank at her anchor in Provincetown Harbor the early morning of November 27. Four men, who were quickly approaching collapse after having been in the shrouds for 15 hours, crept down from the rigging as the life-savers arrived. The lifeless body of the captain's father was lashed in the rigging.*
- Juanita ~ *This vessel, less than a year old, was blown ashore at Cohasset, MA. Her crew escaped in the dories; all survived.*
- King Phillip, Cape Cod
- Knott V. Martin, (schooner) Cape Ann / Marblehead, MA
- Leander V. Beebe (schooner), Boston Bay / Greenport, NY
- Leora M. Thurlow, Vineyard Sound
- Lester A. Lewis (schooner), Wood End, MA / Bangor, ME / 5 ~ *Sank in Provincetown Harbor the early morning of November 27. Her crew took refuge in the rigging, where they perished before help could arrive.*
- Lexington (schooner), New Shoreham, RI

183

- Lillian, Portland, ME
- Lizzie Dyas (schooner), Boston Bay
- Lucy A. Nickels (bark), Point Allerton, MA / Searsport, ME / 5 ~ *Wrecked by the hurricane on Black Rock. In attempting to swim to the rock, the master and mate was drowned. The other members of the crew found in a gunning hut on the rock. The vessel was a wreck and one of the survivors seriously injured.*
- Lucy Bell (schooner), Boston Bay / Patchogue, NY
- Lucy Hammond (schooner), Vineyard Sound / Machias, ME
- Lunet (schooner), Naushon Island, MA / Calais, ME

Albert Butler

- Luther Eldridge (schooner), Nantucket / Chatham, MA
- M. and A. Morrison (schooner), Herring Cove, MA
- Marion Draper (schooner), Vineyard Sound / Bath, ME
- Mary Cabral, Cape Cod
- Mary Emerson, Boston Bay
- Mascot (cat), Cuttyhunk, MA / Gloucester, MA
- M. E. Eldridge, Vineyard Sound
- Mertis H. Perry (fishing schooner), Brant Rock, MA / Joshua Pike/14 ~ *Dashed ashore 2 mi. NNW of the life-saving station between 9-10:00 a.m. on November 27. 5 men were lost. The conditions of the weather were such that it was impossible for the life-savers to discover the vessel when she came ashore, much less reach her in time to save lives.*
- Michael Henry, Cape Cod
- Mildred and Blanche, Cape Cod
- Milo (sloop), Boston Bay / Boston, MA
- Multnoman, Portsmouth, NH
- Nautilus, Cape Cod
- Nellie B. (sloop), New Shoreham, RI

- Nellie Doe (schooner), Vineyard Sound / Bangor, ME
- Nellie M. Slade (bark), Vineyard Sound / New Bedford, MA
- Neptune, Portland, ME
- Neverbuge (cat), Cuttyhunk, MA
- Newburg, Vineyard Sound
- Newell B. Hawes (schooner), Plum Island, MA / Wellfleet, MA / 5 ~ *Driven ashore during the gale and snowstorm and fetched up near the lighthouse. Surfmen worked with the schooner's crew until the 4th of December when they succeeded in floating the vessel.*
- Ohio (steamer), Spectacle Island
- Papetta, Vineyard Sound
- Pentagoet, Cape Cod
- Percy (schooner), New Shoreham, RI
- Phantom, Boston Bay
- Philomena Manta (schooner), Cape Cod / Provincetown, MA / lost on fishing banks of MA Feb 1905)
- Pluscullom Bonum (schooner), Boston Bay / Boston, MA
- Portland, Off Cape Cod
- Powder vessel (steamer), N. Scituate, MA
- Queen of the West (schooner), Fletcher's Neck, ME / 2 ~ *Wrecked on Fletchers Neck. Both crewmen and a dog brought off safely.*
- Quesay, Vineyard Sound
- Rebecca W. Huddell (schooner), Vineyard Sound / Philadelphia, PA
- Reliance (cat), Point of Woods, NY
- Rendo, Portland, ME
- Rienzi (schooner), Cape Ann / Sedgwick, ME
- Ringleader, Portsmouth, NH
- Robert A. Kennier (schooner), Boston Bay / NY NY
- Rose Brothers (schooner), New Shoreham, RI / Newport, RI
- Rosie Cobral, Boston Bay
- S.F. Mayer, Rockland, ME
- Sadie Wilcutt, Vineyard Sound
- Sarah, Cape Ann
- School Girl (schooner), Cape Cod / Provincetown, MA

- Schooner (unknown), Boston Bay
- Schooner (unknown), Boston Bay
- Schooner (unknown), Boston Bay
- Schooner (unknown), Boston Bay
- Schooner (unknown), Cape Cod
- Schooner (unknown), Cape Cod
- Secret (cat), Cuttyhunk, MA
- S. E. Raphine (downeast lumberman), Boston Bay
- Silver Spray, Portland, ME
- Sloop (unknown), Boston Bay
- Sloop (unknown), Boston Bay
- Sloop (unknown), White Head, ME
- Sport (cat), Cuttyhunk, MA / Boston, MA
- Startle (sloop), Boston Bay / NY NY
- Stranger (cat), New Shoreham, RI
- Sylvester Whalen (schooner), Cape Cod / Boston, MA
- T.W. Cooper (schooner), Portsmouth, NH / Machias, ME
- Tamaqua (ocean tug), Boston Bay
- Thomas B. Reed, Cape Cod

FAST ON ROCKS.

Steamer Fairfax on Sow and Pigs Shoals.

All Night Battling With the Gale, Bound to Boston.

- Two Sisters, Portsmouth, NH
- Two-Forty, Boston Bay
- Union, Boston Bay
- Unique, Cape Cod
- Unknown vessel, Boston Bay
- Valetta, Vineyard Sound
- Valkyrie (sloop), New Shoreham, RI
- Verona (schooner), Boston Bay / Cleveland, OH
- Vigilant, Cape Cod
- Virginia (downeast lumberman), Boston Bay
- W.H. DeWitt, Cape Ann
- W.H.Y. Hackett (Schooner), Portsmouth, NH
- Watchman (downeast lumberman), Boston Bay
- Wild Rose (schooner), Cranberry Isles, ME ~ *Stranded and sunk in a terrific gale. Crew safely taken off board.*

- William Leggett, Cape Ann
- William M. Wilson (schooner), Wachapreague, VA / 6 ~ *Sprung a leak and sank 3 miles NNE of station. Surfmen set out to her assistance by hauling the boat along the beach, it being impossible to pull out to her from the station. They saw the crew from Metomkin Inlet Station sail out to her and take off the crew.*
- William Todd, Vineyard Sound

References

Boston News-Letter, Aug. 15, 1720.

The Vial Poured Out upon the Sea,.

Boston News-Letter, Nov. 14, 1720;

Boston Gazette, Oct. 24-31, 1720

Expedition Whydah, by Barry Clifford with Paul Perry

Finding New England's Shipwrecks and Treasure, by Robert Ellis Cahill

Historic Storms of New England: Its Gales, Hurricanes, Tornadoes, Showers ... By Sidney Perley

Boston Globe, August 24, 1986 and June 2, 1906.

Harwich Independent

CapeCodLinks.com

NationalGeographic.com

Harwich Vessels 1872 – 1900, 1998

tinpan.fortunecity.com

thefreedictionary.com

U-Boat.net

U.S. Life-Saving Service Annual Reports

National Maritime Museum, London

Wikipedia –the Free Encylopedia

Truro: The Story of a Cape Cod Town - Richard F. Whalen

U S Coast Guard *Golden Tide Rips* – 1953

Naval Institute Proceedings (Vol 127).

Life Savers of Cape Cod 1904 J W Dalton – Frank Akerman

New England Magazine; an Illustrated Monthly - Volume 31

Annual Report of the Operations of the United States Lifesaving Service – 1878

Boston Daily Globe, June 16, 1913

The Lightships of Nantucket Sound, Thomas Leach, Harbormaster Harwich, Massachusetts, January 2006

Life savers of Cape Cod, John Wilfred Dalton -1902

Books by Theodore Parker Burbank

- ➤ Pirates and Treasure in New England
- ➤ Pirates and Treasure on Cape Cod
- ➤ Shipwrecks, Pirates and Treasure in Maine
- ➤ A Homeowner's Complete Guide to Energy Independence
- ➤ The "Islands" of Ocean Bluff and Brant Rock
- ➤ 365 Ways to Unplug Your Kids or *How to have fun without TV or Computers*
- ➤ A Guide to Plymouth's Famous Burial Hill
- ➤ A Cookbook for UNLUCKY Fishermen or *How to Cook Bait*

Need an entertaining speaker?

Ted is available to provide your club or organization a presentation on any of the subjects covered by his books (except maybe "How to Cook Bait) or to participant in your pirate festival or fair.

Ted Burbank

Call: 508.794.1200 to schedule

31758773R00116

Made in the USA
Charleston, SC
28 July 2014